The Art of Life:

Studies in American Autobiographical Literature

By Mutlu Konuk Blasing

University of Texas Press Austin & London

PS
169
A95
B5

3/1977
Am. Lit.

Permission to reprint material from the following works is gratefully acknowledged:

Chapter One, "The Economies of *Walden*," is reprinted in modified form from *Texas Studies in Literature and Language* 17, no. 4 (Winter 1976): 759–775. Reprinted by permission of the University of Texas Press.

Collected Earlier Poems, by William Carlos Williams. © 1938 by New Directions Publishing Corp. Reprinted by permission of New Directions Publishing Corp.

Collected Later Poems, by William Carlos Williams. © 1944 by William Carlos Williams. Reprinted by permission of New Directions Publishing Corp.

The Collected Poems of Frank O'Hara, edited by Donald Allen. © 1971 by Alfred A. Knopf, Inc. Reprinted by permission of Alfred A. Knopf, Inc.

Paterson, by William Carlos Williams. © 1946, 1948, 1949, 1951, 1958, by William Carlos Williams. Reprinted by permission of New Directions Publishing Corp.

The Poems of Emily Dickinson, edited by Thomas H. Johnson, Cambridge, Massachusetts. The Belknap Press of Harvard University Press, © 1951, 1955, by the President and Fellows of Harvard College. Reprinted by permission of the publisher and the Trustees of Amherst College.

The publication of this book was assisted by a grant from the Andrew W. Mellon Foundation.

Library of Congress Cataloging in Publication Data

Blasing, Mutlu Konuk, 1944–
    The art of life.
    Bibliography: p.
    Includes index.
    1. American literature—History and criticism. 2. Autobiography.
I. Title.
PS169.A95B5   810'.9   76-20760
ISBN 0-292-70315-5

Set by G & S Typesetters, Inc.

Illustrations by Ed Lindlof

To Randy

Contents

Acknowledgments ix

Introduction. The Form of History
and the History of Form xi

1. The Economies of *Walden* 1

2. "Walt Whitman, a Kosmos, of
Manhattan the Son" 25

3. Henry James's Prefaces, or
the Story of the Stories 55

4. Henry Adams, Connoisseur of Chaos 77

5. Two Poets 113
Paterson: Notes toward an American
Revolution 117
Frank O'Hara and the Poetics of Love 139

Coda. New Life in a New World 157

Notes 161

Sources Cited 177

Index 187

Acknowledgments

This study began at Brown University under the auspices of the American Civilization Program; a postdoctoral fellowship in American literature from the University of Massachusetts at Amherst enabled me to complete it. I am thankful to Brown University and the University of Massachusetts for their support.

Professors David H. Hirsch and George Monteiro read most of this study, and I am grateful for their advice and encouragement. I also wish to thank Holly Carver of the University of Texas Press for her help and Randy Blasing for his many suggestions along the way.

Introduction
The Form of History and
the History of Form

A GOOD PART of American literature may be characterized as autobiographical, and while this study is not a survey of American autobiography, it is to a certain extent an examination of autobiographical literature in America. In choosing to consider Henry David Thoreau's *Walden*, Walt Whitman's "Song of Myself," Henry James's Prefaces, Henry Adams's *The Education of Henry Adams*, William Carlos Williams's *Paterson*, and the poetry of Frank O'Hara, I have tried both to represent the variety of autobiographical literature and to indicate a corresponding variety of approaches to it. As my choice of examples suggests, the term "autobiographical" here does not imply any particular standard of "truth" to the "facts," since the recording of a life necessarily represents the fictionalization—to a greater or lesser degree—of the life lived. In my usage, "autobiographical" refers to works in which the hero, narrator, and author can be identified by the same name. I am not interested so much in the motivations of strictly autobiographical recordings as in the structures and dynamics of writers' creating literature out of their historical selves.

This interest has led me to choose *Walden* and "Song of Myself" as my starting points. Yet the predominance of the autobiographical mode in American literature suggests that this subject is in some way distinctively American, and the works that I study are related to earlier manifestations of the autobiographical impulse in Puritan spiritual autobiographies, on the one hand, and in Benjamin Franklin's story of his archetypal worldly progress, on the other. As various readers have pointed out, a work like *Walden*— with its innerness and all-consuming self-consciousness— can be traced back to a work like Jonathan Edwards's

Personal Narrative. But this is not all of *Walden*: the Thoreau persona is also a shrewd, calculating Yankee, who is closer to a Ben Franklin than to an Edwards. "Song of Myself" has likewise been placed in the tradition of Puritan and Quaker spiritual autobiographies. Yet "Song of Myself" is also an expression of an extremely fluid environment and the archetypal chameleonlike hero that this environment inspires—a process first enacted and recorded by Franklin's elusive hero.

The range of such possible connections suggests that in tracing a tradition of personal literature in America one is dealing less with direct influences and more with a series of responses to essentially similar social, spiritual, and literary experiences. For example, the enduring fluidity of the American environment fosters a kind of isolation that makes the writer turn inward and explore, as Thoreau puts it, "the Atlantic and Pacific Ocean of one's being alone." *where?* At the same time, the writer's relation to the reader has to become more or less didactic, as the inner experience— sometimes its very inwardness itself—becomes a public example in being communicated. In this way, autobiography has proved to be a congenial form for American writers, because it asserts both their spiritual power to create or regenerate themselves and their potentially political power to change hearts and minds. The two strains of American autobiography—the spiritual or religious and the worldly or political—come together in Thoreau and Whitman, who offer us simultaneously spiritual instruction and worldly lessons in survival. The two kinds of instruction are inseparable in Thoreau and Whitman because their exemplary personal experiences were not their sole way of communicating some truth that transcended the history of the self. Instead, the self—the "simple separate person"—and its history and communication had become their literary subject, their American material. Unlike Edwards or Franklin, then, Thoreau and Whitman were primarily artists and saw themselves as such.

I have chosen to begin this study with the first examples

of autobiographical literature that we have, for my purpose is not to provide a definitive theory of autobiography in America but to define the critical approaches that autobiographical literature demands. Indeed, my primary purpose is to develop a method of talking about literature as a totality—a method that would render terms like "subject," "form," and "style" exactly convertible to each other. Autobiographical literature is particularly suited to my purpose, for it reveals the dynamics of its creation more readily than other kinds of literature and thereby gives us a chance to observe the literary work as the whole that it is at its inception. I intend, then, to explore the process of creation—the process by which history becomes conscious and consciousness becomes form. And autobiography actually enacts the conversion of history into form not just once but continuously, because the "I" in its self-consciousness constitutes at the same time the historical subject, the shaping form, and the personalizing style of autobiography.

Thus autobiographical literature has the status of a metaliterature, because it reveals the process by which history and form become convertible. As literature, such a work embodies a dialog with its tradition and models—with the history of its form and language. For example, *The Education of Henry Adams* is deliberately cast as a conscious dialog with its tradition, for it represents a completion of Saint Augustine's *Confessions*, a rebuttal of the *Confessions* of Jean Jacques Rousseau, and an inversion of *The Autobiography of Benjamin Franklin*. Moreover, part of the significance of works like *Walden*, "Song of Myself," and *Paterson* derives from their experimental forms, which embody their respective dialogs with English and American literary tradition. Even an apparently unprecedented undertaking like James's Prefaces may be seen in the context of such models as Dante's *La Vita Nuova*, Poe's "The Philosophy of Composition," and Hawthorne's and Melville's various prefaces, for any literary work exists as a dialog with tradition, whether this dialog is consciously articulated or not.

We could say that the history of literature represents a continual self-transcendence—a continual surpassing of what has become convention.[1] Yet the momentum of form alone cannot explain the departures from tradition that make for art. The fact that a particular departure or transformation becomes conceivable, possible, or necessary at a given time attests to the artist's involvement in another dialog, which is extraformal and has its own momentum. This second dialog is with history or with the artist's temporal experience in the context of his or her perception of the total collective experience. As such, the artist's history includes his or her consciousness or the very appropriation and transcendence of history; as a result, we could even speak of an antiformal dialog and regard the work as a clash between the conservatism of form and the radical nature of consciousness, which exists as continuous change and self-transcendence. The literary work, then, may be seen either as form informing history or as history transforming form.

Autobiography records this transaction while enacting it. To begin with, the subject of autobiographical writing is the self becoming conscious of itself in and as history. Although this statement most obviously characterizes *Paterson* and O'Hara's poems, it applies equally to the most closed work under consideration. The Prefaces of Henry James also constitute a transformation of the private self into a public hero, since the simple act of self-consciousness itself involves the recognition of oneself as representative and, therefore, as functioning in and as history. After all, recognition of one's identity as consciousness attests to one's identity with all conscious beings. Second, the inclusive form of autobiography embodies the interaction of history and consciousness. The "I" becomes the organizing principle, for it is in being perceived by the "I" that diverse phenomena become related. Moreover, the "I" provides not only the formal center but the very form of the work. For example, the cyclical progression of *Walden*, the self-transcending evolution of "Song of Myself," the self-destructive degeneration of *The Education of Henry Adams*, and the "dissipation" of *Paterson* are formal patterns that reflect exactly the personal needs of their respective authors. Finally, style is not only self-expressive but has a historical function as well: as O'Hara's career demonstrates most dramatically, it is style that makes the "I" an "I"—a continuous, publicly enduring entity. Thus, although subject, form, and style in autobiography are so many mirrors reflecting each other, it is also true that autobiography transcends this solipsism, for not only has the self-recording consciousness developed within a particular historical context, but the formal patterns and the style that shape and reshape this development, as well as the narrative and the language that record it, are modes of organization and communication that are shared by the culture as a whole. Autobiography, then, represents a self-examination that is at the same time private and public, for the interaction of personality and collective life that autobiography embodies is reflected in the author's personal appropriation of the language of the times. Since autobiography thus bridges public and private life, the hero of autobiography is the paradoxical private-person-as-public-hero. As we shall see, it is in being communicated or in being made public that introspection—the inner ordeal—becomes heroic. Therefore, just as history becomes conscious and achieves form in autobiography, consciousness itself becomes history in achieving form.

Since the subject and form of autobiography meet in the historical experience of its author-hero, the genre naturally remains quite protean. As the variety of my examples illustrates, the forms of its expression are created by each writer out of personal needs. Thus autobiographical literature is particularly suitable for a study of the interaction of history and form, because it is this kind of literature that retains the closest ties to its roots as a space-time event. If a literary work is seen as an event, history and literature, content and form, and public language and style become useless distinctions. Maurice Merleau-Ponty complains that the Museum detaches works of art from the chance circumstances of their creation and leads us to believe that the artist's hand was guided from the start by fate: "the Museum converts this secret, modest, non-deliberated, involuntary, and, in short, living historicity [of the creation] into official and pompous history."[2] Similarly, Jean-Paul Sartre accuses the Library of making "messages" of what were originally gestures. This kind of transformation, which alienates the work from its historicity and its life as an event and makes of it a "relic," parallels the dissection of the work into form, content, language, and style. Yet Merleau-Ponty's statement needs to be qualified. If we approach the completed work as we approach any past event, the work will be seen to consist of both freedom and fate. Only within the context of fate can the past be retrieved *as* the set of possibilities that it was, not simply because it has already become an undeniable present but because only the present—the fate of the past—can provide a clue to the range of past possibilities. Thus the completed form may be seen as the fate of the work's historicity. Just as autobiography records the conversion of history into form, as literature it also embodies this conversion in reverse, since its form is necessarily historical. As a result, autobiography bridges art and history and represents a denial both of art as an absolute activity and of history as metaphor and meaning. Art and history are thereby personalized, and the experience of time is reintroduced as the center of each. Thus I am interested in finding an approach that would relate writers as persons in history to their art and, at the same time, would stay clear of psychological and historical interpretations alike. While the psychological emphasis discounts the public history and the function of art as rhetoric, the historian's approach subordinates the private history and the private problems that the work creates as well as solves. Moreover, both of these approaches minimize the momentum of form or the dialog with its tradition that the work embodies; an ideal approach would attempt to comprehend this dialog also.

Seen as event, literature reverts to drama or, more accurately, to ritual. In autobiographical literature as ritual, the artist may be seen to enter into formal communication both with the age or history and with the past, which includes literary tradition as well as one's personal past. As each of the works under consideration demonstrates, autobiography provides one with a way of placing oneself in history. If we regard literature as formal communication, however, we can no more use it to learn about its age than we can account for its forms with our knowledge of the period, since as a ritual experience the literary work exists as the confluence of public *and* private significances. The work represents the point at which a particular relation between the self and the collective experience can be marked in—and preserved from—time, for the time structure that a literary work creates makes a niche in time and marks a point or moment, much as a cathedral makes its mark not only in the space of art history but in geographical or real space. Similarly, the point that the literary work marks in historical time is essentially nonrepeatable, but the point that it marks in physical time is repeatable even now, because physical time is always present. As in ritual, then, the originating context and experience are essentially nonrepeatable, because they arise from a subjective appreciation of a particular moment in time. As form, however, the literary experience is eminently repeatable, because the work is equally accessible to all users of its language. When the literary work is seen as formal communication, even content becomes form—that is, it becomes a *locus of events* and ceases being particular and unique. It is for this reason that a single form is able to accommodate diverse experiences or events. When seen as history, each experience is unique; when seen as form, it becomes similar to a whole class of experiences. As a result, literature requires very few forms in order to make a limited number of statements again and again. Yet each form is always discovered anew, because each statement is always arrived at personally out of each writer's needs.

When we regard literature as a ritual event, we can reconcile the idea of art as a response to a specific historical —psychological and public—context or as a "strategy for living"[3] and the idea of art as drama or as a purely formal conversion of private time into history. As ritual event or, more simply, as gesture, the work has a historical context but a repeated and repeatable form. Susanne Langer sees ritual as originating in "gestures," which are "natural actions" transformed into formal actions through self-conscious repetition. Similarly, we could say that in being transformed into art the artist's acts become gestures. As such, the artist's acts become deliberate, for they are no longer, in Langer's terms, "emotional *acts*" that are "subject to spontaneous variation"; instead, they are "bound to an often meticulously exact repetition, which gradually makes their forms as familiar as words or tunes."[4] Thus the artist's act is transformed from emotional expression into pure drama and thereby becomes *our* ritual. Although the experience in drama is formally and objectively defined and delimited, its reenactment, which represents its fulfillment, is necessarily an experience in the history of the reader, and its significance, therefore, is necessarily subjective.

In this way, art comes to transform history, which is the avowed enemy, so to speak, of anyone who writes autobiography. And history ranges from being simply unreal in the experience of Thoreau and Whitman to being a nightmare in the extreme experience of Adams. Unreal and chaotic, history is a dream, for in its essence it escapes the mind's grasp—that is, in its essence it is unrepeatable. Only temporal phenomena that repeat themselves and thus coincide with biological time can be appropriated as myth. History becomes myth only upon being abstracted into repeatable messages, and since repetition itself is cohesive, history-as-myth makes for cultural cohesion. This transformation of history into myth constitutes the basis of cultural identity in America, and Whitman's poetry, for example, is partly a response to and partly responsible for this mythicizing of history. Autobiographical literature represents one more attempt to make the unrepeatable repeatable or, in other words, to make the uniqueness of history partake of the recurrence of myth.

As literature, then, the autobiographical work is dramatic in its repeatable form; as semihistorical recording, however, it is a strategy for living, for its subject is the repetition of one's life. D. H. Lawrence writes that "one sheds one's sickness in books—repeats and presents again one's emotions, to be master of them."[5] Yet repetition is curative in a more basic way. By reliving the passively suffered dream of history, one makes it real and comprehensible, since repeating one's history is a way of mastering it. For this reason, Freud regards repetition compulsion as stronger than even the pleasure principle; however painful the experience that one once suffered passively, one is compelled to relive it over and over in order to master the situation.[6] This compulsion, which may be seen, say, in children's playing doctors or teachers and thereby actively mastering unpleasant situations, informs the autobiographical impulse as well. For example, Whitman's catalogs represent his attempts to come to terms with the disorder and the discrepancies in what he perceives, for the catalogs retain something of the chaotic element that initially made his experience less than totally pleasurable. Similarly, twentieth-century urban poets like Williams and O'Hara also repeat in their work what most resists mastery—the chaos, violence, and speed of city life. Moreover, from Thoreau's re-cycling of nature in his *Journal* and *Walden* to James's minute re-visionings and Adams's reconstruction of his career, this mastery through repetition is the object of autobiographical writing. When the particulars or facts of history form a system of relations in a work of art, they become repeatable and therefore constitute a comprehensible experience. On the other hand, old newspapers, for example, are unreadable and essentially incomprehensible, because the particulars remain too close to their roots in the chaos of history.

The relations that autobiography establishes do not necessarily derive from an external system or theory that is imposed on experience; instead, the life simply *is* this particular configuration of these particulars. Thus the relations between experiences are historical or temporal relations, and temporality organizes as well as informs the experience in autobiography. For autobiography is not a static meditation on the self. As Roy Pascal argues, the self is so elusive that it can be grasped only through a historical narrative, not analytically.[7] Although Whitman, for example, rejects narrative in favor of an evolutionary progression, even he employs a historical or temporally irreversible order in shaping his history. The relations, then, are those of the telling; or since the telling, the style, the form, and the person are one in autobiography, the relations are those that personality establishes, and particulars that are related to a personality are related to each other. Since the repetition is formal, however, and since the relations are established in language, they are not private relations. Not only does their significance become public, but they *are* public at their very inception, for language and the structures of narrative embody connections and patterns of relation that are shared by the entire culture.

In making history repeatable, art denies time. Like science and the writing of history, art is a ruse for escaping history, because it works with repeatable time. As a result, the novel is, in Roland Barthes's words, "a Death; it transforms life into destiny, a memory into a useful act, duration into an orientated and meaningful time."[8] This statement, which O'Hara's "In Memory of My Feelings" corroborates for poetry, applies equally to autobiography, which in the hands of Thoreau and Adams actually becomes an anticipation of death. As repetition-in-reverse, however, anticipation represents another strategy for gaining control over history. For instance, Whitman masters the future by anticipating in the 1855 "Song of Myself" the very person he was to become. Similarly, when James recollects his career in the Prefaces and sees himself as anticipating all along the artist that he has become, he is mastering his past. Autobiography, then, is repetition: either it repeats life, as, say, in the case of Adams, or life repeats it, as in the case of Whitman. Better yet, as Thoreau, James, and Williams illustrate, both processes go on simultaneously.

The principle of repetition also informs the peculiar economy or essential narcissism of autobiography. Beginning with the Romantic period, poets see their authority diminish and their range of subjects shrink to the extent that, eventually, they can speak only about themselves. When one casts oneself as the center of reality, however, one becomes committed to continuous self-scrutiny. For the "phantom of life" that the poet seeks resides nowhere; like Narcissus, the poet knows that should one turn away from this incessant self-contemplation, one would become no one. Consequently, the poet or author has to turn to personal literature, in which author, narrator, and hero—one's form, style, and subject—become mirrors contemplating and endlessly repeating each other. As a result, repetition becomes a structural or an organizational principle as well. Yet this literary solipsism, which reflects Narcissus's straits, is potentially self-destructive. And the death wish that informs Narcissus's experience informs as well the experience of the autobiographer, for the wish to return to an inorganic state is, in Freud's terms, the ultimate expression of the repetition compulsion.⁹ Moreover, in transforming life into destiny—in resurrecting the past as necessary —autobiographers in effect anticipate death, because they deny their continuing historical natures in order to repeat the past. Anticipating death, however, is a strategy for overcoming it, and the author plays dead, so to speak, only in order to be reborn. It is for this reason that each of the works to be considered—even as suicidal a work as *The Education of Henry Adams*—ends on a note of resurrection.

As event, then, autobiographical literature becomes a strategy for transcending one's historical essence. Seen as gesture, however, literature itself becomes part of history. If history is life becoming conscious of itself as time, as self-consciousness autobiographical literature creates this consciousness of time. In this way, such literature makes for history, not only for the individual but for the public or the culture that literature thereby helps to create. In the first place, narrative—or historically organized art in general—may be said to *create* a historical mode of perception, for when events are arranged in a temporal order they assume temporal relationships. Since language itself is a temporal medium, a narrative order may be seen as the refinement or the formalization of a general tendency of language itself. It is in poetry that the temporal nature of language is most fully exploited; just as sculpture and architecture create the sense of space, poetry may be said to create the very consciousness of time, for it is in poetry that time becomes functional. The fact that history began as narrative poetry attests to the idea that literature creates a historical mode of perception or experience. Furthermore, literature creates its *occasion* as history, for it is through literature that diverse phenomena occurring at a given time become a happening and constitute a moment. Thus the age congeals and becomes whole; the Transcendental age, the period of *fin de siècle*, and the Modern era, for example, are defined by the art that composed them.

Moreover, the work of art places itself in, and becomes part of, the history that it serves partly to create. The work of art is historical in a number of ways. First, we may apply Marcel Duchamp's view of art to works of literature. In his view, the work is not an object to which one reacts, but a "temporary center of energy which gives rise to psychic events." The work of art, then, is like an "irradiated substance," and only when its "charge" dies down does it begin to "*last*."[10] In becoming historical, moreover, art escapes the Museum. As Harold Rosenberg suggests, although self-destructive works of art like happenings and earth works would appall a Duchamp, these developments are really extensions of Duchamp's idea of art as history. To a certain extent, self-destructive art represents a rebellion against both the possessiveness of the art public and the politics of the galleries; by escaping the Museum, however, art reveals its vulnerability, for the guise of fatedness is the protection that the Museum affords art. The idea that art enjoys a privileged position outside history derives from the concept of art as a necessary or fated activity. In renouncing these ideas of art, the artist becomes conscious of the arbitrariness of art. It is this awareness that troubles someone like James and leads him to construct, as it were, his own Museum—a superstructure that uses the art itself as its matériel. Frank O'Hara's poetry, which in some ways represents an extreme of autobiographical writing, likewise attests to a consciousness of the arbitrariness of art. In O'Hara's "Personism," each poem becomes the locus of an event—the point at which the inner and outer histories momentarily converge to define a truly historical self. Of course, such historical poetry may be abandoned to the confusion of history once its charge dies down —that is, after it has served as a "psychic event." This idea of the poem as historical event accounts for the unapologetically personal—not private—nature of O'Hara's poetry and explains his possibly cultivated carelessness with his poems, which he sometimes carried to the extent of not even keeping copies.

Second, just as the work of art has a private history, it also has a public history. The role of art in collective life is essentially cohesive, for the work creates its occasion as history at its inception and continues to make history each time it is read. According to Henri Focillon, the histories of the different expressions of collective life unfold at different speeds;[11] for example, the rate of industrial change is not the same as the rate of change in the arts. A work of art, however, creates a moment or a "now" point which intersects all these continua. Using *Walden* as an example, we may regard it as a "now" point that represents a particular cross section of the continua of politics, economics, religion, American literature, and the humanizing or denaturing of the American environment at the time of its writing. Since these continua have different rates of progress, *Walden* today represents a very different cross section than it did in 1854, and it cannot be used to discover the particular cross section of 1854. *Walden* as a "now" point —as pure form—is a continually changing set of contents, and in order to discover the particular configuration that it represented in 1854, we would need independent knowledge of the period, which we would then try to match with the book. The only way that *Walden* can serve the purposes of a historian is by providing—at the time that it is under examination—a temporary center around which the accumulated historical facts may be organized. For whenever it is created or experienced, a work of art provides a stasis or a point in time at which the various continua that make up collective life are momentarily arrested in a particular relationship. It is in art, then, that experience becomes conscious, because the personal experience of the writer or reader can enter into a formal relationship with the collective experience.

Regarding a work as history also enables us to account for the changes of the work itself. Throughout its history a work accumulates perspectives and interpretations, takes on increasingly larger significance, and grows more and more multifarious. In other words, a work becomes the sum of its readings and contains, in a sense, not only numerous readers but all the years of its existence. Since a work is not a historical object or an antique but a living thing or, even, history itself, what it says to each reader and each age is its *true* nature, which—like all historical entities— is continuously evolving. Whatever the author may have "really meant," then, is of specialized, even antiquarian, interest only.

Finally, a literary work has its own temporal structure, which embodies the life span of a consciousness. Since the form of a work is an internal temporal structure, all the changes that the work undergoes in the hands of different readers are changes within the limits of its first and last

words, because there is no time before the work begins and
no time after it ends. As Alain Robbe-Grillet claims about
his "new novel," art is all "presence," for a novel is not a
slice of time from a time continuum that exists outside the
work but a complete time structure; when the work ends,
therefore, time ends.[12] The time span of a work of literature represents a total cycle of consciousness, and this
cycle of consciousness—this birth, growth, and death—
constitutes its form.

Autobiography, however, is an open-ended genre, which
posits a time before and after the work as part of the fiction itself. Yet when Thoreau, Whitman, James, and Adams transform autobiography into art, they compensate
for the open-endedness of their form by completing their
stories. For example, Thoreau isolates a span of years in
Walden and makes them emblematic of a life cycle, complete with rebirth. More ambitious, Whitman encompasses
a lifetime in "Song of Myself" and justifies his project by
expanding Thoreau's natural life cycle into a mythic life
cycle. James completes his form by writing his last Preface
or the "story" of the story of the stories, and he also enacts the end of his life. Since his life is equated with his
career, the writing of the Prefaces, which shows the career
to be over, suggests that in a sense life, too, is over. Adams
perfects this kind of suicidal maneuver in *The Education
of Henry Adams* when he addresses us from beyond the
grave, so to speak. On the other hand, Williams's and
O'Hara's more impure conceptions of art enabled them to
live with the open-endedness of their forms. For example,
after bidding his reader a formal good-by at the end of
Book 4 of *Paterson* with "This is the blast / the eternal
close / . . . the end," Williams refuses to let well enough
alone and adds a fifth book to *Paterson* and even projects a
sixth, simply because he is still living and thinking about
the same things. Art is no more sacred to O'Hara; he ends
"In Memory of My Feelings" with the announcement that
it is time for the poem to end and for the time after the
poem to begin.

reader-
author

When literature is seen as ritual, the reader assumes her or his properly creative role. As event, autobiography calls out for an auditor who will complete or seal it. The "I" and the "you" whom the "I" addresses are both on stage; consequently, the work should not be seen as an object, because one cannot simply speak for oneself. Whom else one is speaking for depends upon which stage one is speaking from, what the props are, and who one's audience is. Sincerity, which is a significant issue in autobiographical writing, should therefore be conceived of dramatically as the aptness of the attitude struck for the particular purposes and the particular audience at hand. It is a matter of effects—a matter to be settled between the author and each reader. When the reader is also on stage, he or she must act and try to become the ideal audience that a particular work is addressing. In effect, the reader attempts to become the author's first reader—the author. As ritual experience, literature allows readers to participate—to act and to watch themselves act. This double perspective is built into the ritual experience, since one must view oneself both from within and from without one's immediate history. The perspective from infinity makes of the experience a ritual, while the historical perspective makes of the ritual a personal experience.

This double perspective in the ritual or dramatic experience of reading reflects the double perspective of autobiographical writing in general, for self-consciousness is common to both reading and writing. Both activities involve introspection and, at the same time, transcendence of the private self. Implicit in self-consciousness, then, is the very perspective by which it can be transcended, since one can escape being trapped in one's subjectivity only by being conscious of oneself as partly object. Thus, although self-consciousness is, theoretically, infinitely regressive and therefore infinitely introspective, it also represents a continuous transcendence of introspection, for whatever consciousness is conscious of becomes thereby a part of history. Accordingly, self-consciousness, which defines autobiography, informs its double perspective, because the hero-author of autobiography is, at the same time, both in and out of history. This doubleness appears in each of the works under consideration. In *Walden*, for example, we see an opposition between the unselfconscious Narcissus-hero, who is not separated from his world, and the necessarily self-conscious—indeed, Promethean—author. Similarly, we find in "Song of Myself" a tension between the mythic bard-hero and the historical author. In the Prefaces, we watch James betray his self-consciousness in arguing for the unselfconscious and organic development of his works; his telltale final Preface, moreover, reveals a secondary self-consciousness—his sense of the arbitrariness of the entire project of the Prefaces. In *The Education of Henry Adams*, this doubleness takes the form of a conflict between the hero, who is a not altogether effective actor in history, and the author as observer.

A double perspective is basic to autobiography and informs even the oldest model of modern autobiography. Jean Starobinski remarks of Saint Augustine's *Confessions* that "the double address of the discourse—to God and to the human auditor—makes the truth discursive and the discourse true. Thus may be united, in a certain fashion, the instantaneousness of the confession offered to God and the sequential nature of the explanatory narrative offered to the human intelligence. And thereby are reconciled the edifying motivation and the transcendent finality of the confession."[13] Substituting "consciousness" for "God," we arrive at the modern version of the essential doubleness of the self as both history and consciousness—as immanent and, at the same time, transcendent. Thus, since the self is both the narrative and the creator of the narrative, the very creation of the self in autobiography constitutes its transcendence. The "I" in autobiography, then, is not only past but present, both the observed and the observer, history and historian, hero and poet, form and life. And this peculiarity of autobiographical writing makes autobiography an essentially comic genre, because the authors consider their historical selves—indeed, history itself—from a comic perspective outside history. *Walden*, "Song of Myself," and *The Education of Henry Adams*, in each of which the hero-author is—in Whitman's words—"both in and out of the game" of history, can all be seen as comic works. Even James's Prefaces contain a comic perspective, although James minimizes this doubleness by attempting to formalize the very history of his forms. In fact, repetition —which is the essence of the autobiographical impulse— necessarily creates a double perspective, for in repeating history one is of necessity both in and out of history. The twentieth-century poets Williams and O'Hara consciously exploit this double perspective. Williams juxtaposes "poetic" pieces, found prose, and eyewitness reporting in *Paterson*, and O'Hara constantly reminds us in his poems that he is writing poetry. In Williams and O'Hara, then, art is seen from the perspective of history, and the hero as artist is seen from the perspective of the person in history.

Given this doubleness of autobiographical writing, I attempt to consider these works both from the inside or as history and from the outside or as form. Each chapter focuses primarily on the aspect of autobiographical writing that is most prominent in the work at hand. Although there is traffic between the chapters, it remains for each reader to make the connections between them as explicit as she or he may require. The first chapter deals mainly with the necessary narcissism of autobiography and its economies. Equally central to all the works that are studied is the process by which history becomes myth, and the second chapter is organized around an examination of this process. I then proceed to a discussion of self-consciousness, retrospection, and narrative, which structure each of the works considered. The fourth chapter emphasizes the double perspective of comedy, and the final chapter studies the formal innovativeness of autobiographical writing. Thus each work is treated as a mirror which may reflect other works. I am interested in these ideas to the extent that they enable us to discuss a literary work as a total experience, as an event, or as a locus for the interaction not simply of history and form but of author, reader, and even critic.

Chapter 1
The Economies of *Walden*

IN THE SECOND PARAGRAPH of *Walden*, Henry David Thoreau writes that he requires "of every writer, first or last, a simple and sincere account of his own life."[1] At the same time, Thoreau was the first to admit that he was not entirely faithful to the facts of his experience in *Walden*, and more than one reader has attempted to prove that *Walden* is closer to fiction than to autobiography. Yet such readings are based on too reductive a definition of autobiography,[2] and in order to correct this imbalance we could argue that autobiography is, in fact, the fictionalization of a life lived. Due to the discrepancy in autobiography between the time of the action and the time of the narration, a fictional situation already exists, since the experiencing "I" is being created out of the memory and within the conceptual framework of the recording "I." In the case of *Walden* this process of fictionalization becomes rather complicated, because the recording went through seven different versions before the final version emerged. What we find in *Walden*, then, is not simply a multiple exposure of the kind we see in *The Autobiography of Benjamin Franklin*, but a narrating "I" that is continuously moving through some seven or eight years.[3] If time distorts experience in autobiographical writing, form and meaning—supplied as they are after the experience—tend likewise to falsify facts. Formal symmetry, for example, demanded that Thoreau condense his two years at Walden into one, and "truth" required that he transcend facts; indeed, he laments that he cannot "exaggerate enough even to lay the foundation of a true expression" (p. 324).

If authors manipulate the facts of their experience for the sake of their chosen forms and meanings, readers and critics are similarly selective. Comprehension itself depends on a degree of formalization, and even if a complete transcription of a life were possible, the critic would end up fictionalizing it. Just as the autobiographer has to choose from the facts of the life, the critic would have to select her or his own forms and meanings out of the multiplicity which is the work. The reader's attitudes and expectations, moreover, play a role in determining the content of a particular work. For example, *Walden* has been read as a factual account and as fiction, as a nature book and as a highly symbolic transcendental text, and as a political-economic manifesto and as poetry.

Thus perhaps we should use the term "autobiographical" not to describe how factual the contents of a book are but to designate a form. In this sense *Walden* is autobiographical: it presents a multifaceted self. Thoreau is split into author, narrator, and hero, who in turn have many faces, ranging from Yankee Philosopher to Poet-Prophet. And the author, narrator, and hero—different entities that share the same name and identity—are mirror images of each other; they reflect and thereby realize each other. It is this identity in difference that in my usage distinguishes autobiography from fiction narrated in the first person. Alfred Kazin suggests another distinction; in his view, autobiography allows for a serious cult of self that fiction cannot offer, because autobiography is centered on a single person.[4] Whereas the first-person hero in both fiction and autobiography is total subjectivity, what further distinguishes fiction from autobiography is that in fiction other characters are provided—in Bertil Romberg's words—to "mirror" the hero-narrator, who thereby gains objectivity and social credibility.[5] A comparison of *Walden* with *Moby-Dick*, for example, nicely illustrates this distinction.

Walden should be considered autobiographical, then, because its author, narrator, and hero have the same name, because it is devoted to self-cultivation, and because its other characters do not serve to mirror the hero or to qualify the subjectivity of his point of view. Yet there is a mirror in *Walden*, which serves to rescue the hero from his own consciousness and to provide a model or an ideal by which to shape his experience. Walden Pond—the "perfect forest mirror" (p. 188)—presents Thoreau with a vision of himself that is idealized because it endures. While Thoreau himself has changed, the pond has remained a steady, incorruptible center which gives continuity and shape to his life: "Though the woodchoppers have laid bare first this shore and then that, and the Irish have built their sties by it, and the railroad has infringed on its border, and the ice-men have skimmed it once, it is itself unchanged, the same water which my youthful eyes fell on; all the change is in me. It has not acquired one permanent wrinkle after all its ripples. It is perennially young" (pp. 192–193). Indeed, the whole of nature provides a mirror for Thoreau: "Would you see your mind," he writes, "look at the sky."[6] And Thoreau's autobiographical form embodies his reflective relationship with nature, for *Walden* was for Thoreau yet another mirror, which reflected another ideal—because indestructible —self. As he revised and reworked *Walden*, he continually resurrected himself, and the book—like Walden Pond— was continually reborn.

Thoreau develops his relationship to the pond explicitly in terms of mirror imagery. Walden becomes "a mirror which no stone can crack, whose quicksilver will never wear off, whose gilding Nature continually repairs; no storms, no dust, can dim its surface ever fresh;—a mirror in which all impurity presented to it sinks" (p. 188). In view of such passages, it even seems possible that Thoreau may have been consciously recalling the legend of Echo and Narcissus. Thoreau calls Walden "earth's eye; looking into which the beholder measures the depth of his own nature" (p. 186). Beholding such depths, might one not come to resemble the trees surrounding Walden, each of which "admired itself reflected in the smooth mirror of the lake" (p. 240)? In any case, Thoreau's insistence on the well-like depth and unnatural clarity of Walden suggests Narcissus's "well-deep and silver-clear" forest pool.[7] And Thoreau studying the reflections on the glassy surface of Walden recalls Narcissus, as "Flat on the grass he lay to look deep, deeper / Into two stars that were his eyes." Finally, Emerson observes that Thoreau "delighted in echoes, and said they were almost the only kind of kindred voices that he heard."[8]

The significance of these echoes of the Narcissus legend

becomes clear when we consider Melville's version of the myth: "And still deeper the meaning of that story of Narcissus, who because he could not grasp the tormenting, mild image he saw in the fountain, plunged into it and was drowned. But that same image, we ourselves see in all rivers and oceans. It is the image of the ungraspable phantom of life; and this is the key to it all."[9] If the "phantom of life" is one's own reflection, however, the watch or self-scrutiny must not be abandoned for a single minute, for existence itself is contingent upon self-consciousness. As Ovid writes of Narcissus, "What he had tried to hold resided nowhere, / For had he turned away, it fell to nothing." The beginnings of this kind of self-consciousness go back as far as Saint Augustine and his spiritual autobiography. "O Lord, I am working hard in this field, and the field of my labours is my own self," Saint Augustine writes. "I have become a problem to myself, like land which a farmer works only with difficulty and at the cost of much sweat. For I am not now investigating the tracts of the heavens, or measuring the distance of the stars, or trying to discover how the earth hangs in space. I am investigating myself, my memory, my mind."[10] In the nineteenth century, however, self-consciousness became more than a philosophical stance; it became a philosophical need. "Over Descartian vortices you hover," Melville writes,[11] for when reflection becomes the ground of being, any loss of self-consciousness leads to nothingness or death. Thoreau diagnosed his age correctly when he wrote, "There probably has been no more conscious age than the present" (J, 3: 236).

Not only the need for relentless self-scrutiny but also a certain humility led nineteenth-century artists like Thoreau to personal literature. Wordsworth, for example, writes of *The Prelude*: "It is not self-conceit . . . that has induced me to do this, but real humility; I began the work because I was unprepared to treat any more arduous subject, and diffident of my own powers."[12] Since in the nineteenth century one could no longer pronounce upon the world at large, one was driven—in a defensive strategy—to *choose* to write about oneself alone. And it is in this context that we should try to understand Thoreau's justification for *Walden*: "In most books, the *I*, or first person, is omitted; in this it will be retained; that, in respect to egotism, is the main difference. We commonly do not remember that it is, after all, always the first person that is speaking. I should not talk so much about myself if there were anybody else whom I knew as well" (p. 3). Like Wordsworth, then, Thoreau chose to write about himself not only out of egotism but out of a humility that was as real if not as openly affirmed.

If, for Wordsworth, personal literature remained the only viable form, for the Americans Thoreau and Whitman it became the only possible form. And since, unlike Wordsworth, they did not hold themselves accountable to a literary tradition, they were able to make bolder claims for personal literature. For at the other end of subjectivity one achieves a kind of objectivity: the "I" is the most particular yet most universal of heroes. As pure subjectivity or consciousness, the "I" becomes a form which, like a mirror, gains content only in reflecting a beholder, and just as Walden Pond and *Walden* were mirrors for Thoreau, Thoreau himself becomes a mirror for the reader. Only the reader can fill in the blank, so to speak, and it is for this reason that Thoreau and especially Whitman make such outrageous demands on their readers.

When the self is cast as the hero, even greater self-scrutiny and heightened self-consciousness are required, no longer in order only to satisfy personal and philosophical needs but now to meet aesthetic demands as well. In this reflexive movement we see the roots of the self-conscious, "insincere" art of our century. For *Walden*, as well as the *Journal*, rests on nothing but its own philosophic and artistic self-consciousness. The Thoreau hero exists only as an observer of himself, and, as we shall see, the language of this self-observation is appropriately self-conscious and makes no pretense of spontaneity.

Thoreau's self-mirroring art, then, is narcissistic. Perhaps we can go one step further, however, and suggest not only that Thoreau was writing autobiography in order to satisfy his philosophical needs as a nineteenth-century artist but that he was in fact writing autobiography in a more conventional sense. For the Thoreau who emerges both from *Walden* and the *Journal* and from the opinions of his acquaintances is a Narcissus-hero, and this image continues to be credible, despite the efforts of numerous critics and biographers to dissociate Thoreau from the more unsavory implications of narcissism. Thoreau writes, for example, of falling in love with trees, he continually harps on his friends' finding him "cold," and he makes statements like "genius is inspired by its own works; it is hermaphroditic" (*J*, 11:204) and "perhaps this is the main value of a habit of writing, of keeping a journal,—that so we remember our best hours and stimulate ourselves" (*J*, 3:217).

Such statements are part of the rhetoric of creating a literary persona; yet if we are to believe at all Emerson's and Lowell's portraits of Thoreau, the narcissism seems indeed autobiographical. Emerson, for example, calls him "the bachelor of thought and Nature."[13] It is dangerous, however, to use biography to explain a work of art. If anything, it works the other way around; as Georges Poulet has argued, it is the work that sometimes enables us to understand the biography.[14] This is especially true here, for although we cannot say precisely to what extent, Thoreau as a person was undoubtedly shaped by the practice of his peculiar art. In his case, then, there appears to be a rather close correspondence between his life and his art, and each demonstrates the marvelous economy of narcissism, since neither in his life nor in his art did Thoreau ever turn to any other character. Lowell was not far from the truth when he wrote of Thoreau, "He was not merely solitary, he would be isolated, and succeeded at last in almost persuading himself that he was autochthonous."[15] Thoreau required only his ego and a mirror—nature or art—to reflect it.

There is yet another way the legend of Narcissus leads us to *Walden*. Narcissus loves himself—"Since I / Am what I long for, then my riches are / So great they make me poor,"—yet it is someone else he loves—"O darling boy whose love was my undoing." The story illustrates the paradox of identity that all life through time exhibits: Narcissus and his double are the same, yet they are not, because they are phenomena of different space-times. Narcissus is not fully conscious of this difference, however, because in his universe the world and ego are not separated. Freud's concept of primary narcissism, for example, refers to an ego that embraces the universe and is inseparable from it. Herbert Marcuse notes the paradox that narcissism—seen usually as egotistic withdrawal from reality—here denotes a state of oneness with the universe.[16]

In Thoreau's world, the bond between the ego and the universe has already been severed, and his attempted return to the state of oneness must necessarily be stained with self-consciousness. In Lowell's somewhat harsh terms, "To seek to be natural implies a consciousness that forbids all naturalness forever."[17] Thoreau himself was quite aware of his essential separation from nature as a civilized man, and this separation, as well as the germ of self-consciousness that is planted with it, accounts for the split that he observed within his consciousness: "With thinking," he writes—and here we should think of "reflecting" with the self-consciousness and doubleness that it implies —"we may be beside ourselves in a sane sense. By a conscious effort of the mind we can stand aloof from actions and their consequences. . . . I only know myself as a human entity; the scene, so to speak, of thoughts and affections; and am sensible of a certain doubleness by which I can stand as remote from myself as from another. However intense my experience, I am conscious of the presence and criticism of a part of me, which, as it were, is not a part of me, but spectator, sharing no experience, but taking note of it; and that is no more I than it is you. When the play, it may be the tragedy, of life is over, the spectator goes his way. It was a kind of fiction, a work of the imagination only, so far as he was concerned. This doubleness may easily make us poor neighbors and friends sometimes" (pp. 134–135). Thoreau, then, is a self-conscious Narcissus, and this self-conscious doubleness enables him to experience life and almost simultaneously to formalize it as art for presentation to the spectator.

This creative process leads—again in a reflexive movement—to increased self-consciousness and a heightened sense of separation from the world. If we accept with Thoreau the vision of childhood as a state of harmonious wholeness or oneness of the ego and the world, it is easy to see why he would look back and try to regain this state. And it is partly this alluring vision of a "glory" gone from the earth that Walden Pond reflects: the pond is still "the same water" his "youthful eyes fell on" (p. 193). In the act of searching for and trying to recapture the wholeness of childhood or of youth, however, the author becomes at the same time conscious artist and various fictional selves —from narrator to hero. The act of writing, then, which necessarily splinters the self, itself increases the demand for wholeness. Consequently, Sherman Paul's contention that *Walden* was created out of Thoreau's despair over the fragmentation of his life after 1850[18] must be balanced with J. Lyndon Shanley's argument that Thoreau's alleged loss of faith in life is only a legend and that it is his work after 1851 that is responsible for the joy and confidence of *Walden*.[19]

If we abandon strictly one-way correspondences between life and art, these two views can be reconciled. Kenneth Burke has written of Poe, for example, that his personal difficulties could easily be seen as practical reflections of his literary methods, rather than the other way around. Burke writes: "For though it is true that artists use art, sometimes successfully, sometimes unsuccessfully, to get themselves out of trouble, the practice of art just as often gets artists into trouble."[20] In Thoreau's case, if the practice of his art helped make him whole, at the same time it further divided him, but perhaps one would not have the whole without the rending. For the kind of art that sets out to regain a past wholeness presupposes and demands a separation of the present self from the lost selves that are being recollected.

This division within wholeness recalls the separateness within identity of the Narcissus legend, and the principle of identity-in-difference or repetition informs *Walden* as a whole. As numerous readers have pointed out, Thoreau uses circularity as an organizing principle to develop the theme of the resurrection of the self and nature. By arranging events in circles as formal reflections of each other, Thoreau solves the problem of how to create a whole out of consecutive events in a consecutive medium. To begin with, in "Economy" he relates the events of the book in sequence, and the rest of *Walden* recapitulates this sequence in greater detail. Furthermore, the symbolic structure of *Walden* as a whole is a circle, which begins and ends with spring. Sherman Paul has noted that Thoreau develops the various cycles—of the day, the seasons, civilizations, and consciousness—along the same pattern of rebirth,[21] and Charles Anderson has shown that *Walden* is not simply a large circle but a complex system of cycles and epicycles, with the imagery and the individual chapters themselves developing the same circular pattern.[22]

Since it has been so thoroughly treated elsewhere, the circularity of *Walden* interests us only peripherally. Yet the circle, which is so important for Thoreau and the Transcendentalists in general, is the perfect image of the kind of repetition that concerns us here. For a circle that is traveled in time is a repetition that is also change, since the circle returns to the same point, but in a different time. The starting point to which the circle returns is no longer, in fact, the same point; in other words, a circle in time necessarily becomes a spiral. Thoreau's understanding of the progressive nature of repetition enabled him, for example, to celebrate *each* morning, because every morning it became possible to awaken "to a higher life than we fell asleep from" (p. 89). Repetition, then, is not a denial of time; instead, the possibility of repetition as renewal affirms the passage of time. A repetition outside time would be identity or endless sameness, which is as "sterile" as continual new beginnings. Like echoes and reflections, however, repetition as Thoreau understands it is an affirmation of change and difference. In an echo of the Narcissus legend, Thoreau writes in "Sounds": "The echo is, to some extent, an original sound, and therein is the magic and charm of it. It is not merely a repetition of what was worth repeating in the bell, but partly the voice of the wood" (p. 123). It is the creative nature of repetition, then, that *Walden* embodies and affirms. Thus part of the perfect economy of *Walden* is that its uses for Thoreau, its themes of cyclical rebirth, and its conspicuous images of mirrors and echoes equally elaborate the paradox of identity-in-difference, and all autobiographical writing—which is repetition—reflects on this problem.

If in *Walden* there is a movement outward to plenitude, there is a corresponding movement inward. For if there are doublings and increasings, they are doublings and increasings as of mirror images or reflections. Emblematic of the method of *Walden* is Thoreau's description of the "vegetation" that is formed by the thawing sand in the "deep cut." Here the single form of a leaf becomes the model for all creation: "The Maker of this earth but patented a leaf" (p. 308). Everything from coral, leopards' paws, birds' feet, and butterflies to brains, lungs, bowels, and excrement is seen as a duplication of one basic form. In addition, the flow of the sand illustrates the formation of blood vessels and rivers. And the leaf form, which itself derives from the forms in the clay, grows in significance through more playful repetitions like "we may turn over a new leaf at last" (p. 308). Perry Miller thinks it strange that Thoreau fixes his image of resurrection not on something natural but on something as sterile as the sand in the deep cut. According to Miller, the passage indicates that Thoreau was aware of the ironies of a life—as he meant *his* to be—based on anticipation.[23] It seems to me, however, that the basis of Thoreau's image of rebirth is not something sterile but something simple, integral, and rich in possibilities of proliferation. For him, "the green and flowery spring" (p. 308) would have been too various, too luxurious, and too real a proliferation for comfort. In Thoreau, all increase comes down to repetition—the endless reproducing of one form, whether circles or leaves. Thus the *"extra vagance"* and "exaggeration" of *Walden*, as well as the extravagance of this passage, are countered by "economy" and a call for "simplification," and *Walden* expands and contracts at the same time.

According to this interpretation, "Economy"—which represents the most sustained expression of one of these poles —is central to *Walden*, and critics who try to explain away the chapter as merely a satirical introduction are hardly justified. That "Economy" is, in fact, largely satire does not detract from the credibility of Thoreau's assertions of his own economy. To begin with, the shrewd enterpriser persona of "Economy" helps to establish the credibility of *Walden* as a whole, for such rhetoric offsets the Transcendentalisms of the later chapters. "Economy" plays an even larger role, however, because the material side of Thoreau's experience at Walden is an essential aspect of it. One of the reasons Thoreau went to Walden was to save money, and one of the continuing themes of *Walden* is something very much like "time is money." And Thoreau keeps returning to some of the themes and techniques of "Economy"; for example, the cost accounting in "The Bean-Field" and the John Field episode in "Baker Farm" recall the concerns of "Economy."

Thoreau's use of images of money or precious jewels reflects this preoccupation with the material. Hills are described as "true-blue coins from heaven's own mint" (p. 87), lakes are "like precious stones" (p. 199), and the ice bubbles are "like silvery coins poured from a bag" (p. 247). The entire enterprise itself is described as "some private business" and "trade" with the "Celestial Empire" (pp. 19, 20). Even friendship becomes "cheap": people may or may not have "value" for each other (p. 136). Joseph Molden-hauer reads this prevalence of monetary imagery as part of Thoreau's technique of working with paradoxes. In Molden-hauer's view, such images are ironic, for Thoreau uses them to attach to his way of life "the deep connotations of worth which social involvements and material comforts evoke for the desperate man."[24]

Although Thoreau's irony is unmistakable, it seems to me that the monetary imagery so pervasive in *Walden* should not be read exclusively as a literary strategy. Emerson recalls Thoreau as the kind of man who in fact was carrying on a profitable "trade": walking around Concord, Thoreau would withdraw from "his breast-pocket his diary, and read the names of all the plants that should bloom on this day, whereof he kept account as a banker when his notes fall due."[25] The use of monetary imagery in *Walden* is part of a possessiveness toward nature that Thoreau dis-played in and out of *Walden*. This possessiveness appears even in innocent remarks like "I wish that we might make more use of leaves than we do. Why wait till they are re-duced to virgin mould. Might we not fill beds with them?" (J, 3:63). And we understand what Emerson meant by his reference to Thoreau's "edible religion."[26] "See not the world with the eye of science, which is barren," Thoreau writes, "nor of youthful poetry, which is impotent. But taste the world and digest it" (J, 3:85). Thoreau's untiring recording of natural phenomena should also be seen in this light, for writing *is* possessing: "Why the owner [of the farm] does not know it for many years when a poet has put his farm in rhyme, the most admirable kind of invisible fence, has fairly impounded it, milked it, skimmed it, and got all the cream, and left the farmer only the skimmed milk" (pp. 82–83).

Economy and possessiveness constitute the movement toward contraction in Thoreau and distinguish him from Whitman and even Emerson, who are often so close to Tho-

reau in what they are saying. As we have seen elsewhere in
Thoreau, however, contraction is balanced by a corresponding expansion, and we could use the image of a microscope
to illustrate these movements. For his microscopic vision
contracts in order to expand. Just as a kind of universality emerges from the total subjectivity of Thoreau's "I," his
vision expands at the far end of contraction. In limiting
his needs, for example, he was not taking a vow of poverty;
in Emerson's words, Thoreau "chose to be *rich* by making
his wants few" (italics mine).[27] As the episode with John
Field in "Baker Farm" reveals, this richness is not only
spiritual but quite real. Similarly, as Joseph Wood Krutch
has observed, Thoreau felt a strong pull toward a Puritan
asceticism and the ideals of a strenuous life, discipline, and
work.[28] Yet the self-denial in Thoreau is not an end in itself
but, in fact, enables him to celebrate himself. Just as he
grows rich by becoming poor, he achieves self-celebration
through self-denial. For what he celebrates with Dionysian
abandon—the truth that he cannot state extravagantly
enough—is precisely self-denial or the ideal of contraction,
which he calls purity and at the other end of which he finds
new life.

The concepts of repetition and economy together illuminate Thoreau's technique. To begin with, his peculiar style
exhibits this simultaneous movement toward proliferation
and economy. For example, he relies on puns, double meanings, and word plays not only for humorous effects but for
more serious commentary. David Skwire has compiled a
checklist of word plays in *Walden*,[29] and we should look at
a few of them here in order to indicate Thoreau's range.
The fashionably overdressed are "cooked, of course *à la
mode*" (p. 14); Thoreau is "anxious to improve the nick of
time, and notch it on . . . [his] stick" (p. 17); "when a man
dies he kicks the dust" (p. 68), which combines "kick the
bucket" and "bite the dust"; the needy appeal to one's "*hos-
pitalality*" (p. 152); the luckless fisher belongs to the "ancient sect of Coenobites" (p. 173) or those who "see no

bites"; and "sleepers" underlie, construct, ride, and sometimes even are overridden by the railroad (pp. 92–93).
Thus Thoreau invents words and sayings, plays variations
on expressions, and exploits sounds and the double or even
multiple meanings of words.

Word plays exemplify both the ideas of identity-in-
difference and economy. In puns, not only the words themselves but the objects and situations that they signify become multifaceted, for a play on words is a play on identity. Consequently, a pun is economical, since one word
comes to radiate many meanings. In fact, Freud in *Jokes
and Their Relation to the Unconscious* attributes the pleasure that we derive from word plays to their economy: "The
multiple use of the same material is, after all, only a special case of condensation; play upon words is nothing other
than condensation *without* substitute-formation; condensation remains the wider category. All these techniques are
dominated by a tendency to compression, or rather to saving. It all seems to be a question of economy. In Hamlet's
words: 'Thrift, thrift, Horatio!' " In addition to the verbal
economy of puns, in jokes as release there is the economy
of psychical energy that is normally spent on inhibition or
suppression.[30] A third kind of economy is the economy of
repetition. Playing with similar sounds, the use of multiple
meanings, and the modification of familiar phrases—all of
which are quite common in Thoreau—are devices for rediscovering the familiar where something new was expected. And the pleasure of rediscovering the familiar, which
is similar to the pleasure of rhyme, alliteration, and re-
frains in verse, is the pleasure of repetition. Once again,
Freud associates this kind of pleasure with "a pleasure in
economy" and relates it to the economy of psychical
energy.[31]

Another element of Thoreau's technique in *Walden* is
his use of analogies. The description of the sand foliage on
the railroad bank exemplifies his discovery of analogous
shapes in myriad forms throughout nature. Thoreau also
makes use of microcosm analogies; for example, if we

would circle the globe, he advises us to turn inward and to "explore the private sea, the Atlantic and Pacific Ocean of one's being alone" (p. 321). Similarly, the account of the ants' war suggests analogies not only with universal human situations but with current events. Moreover, analogies provide the organizing principle of the discussion of food, shelter, clothing, and warmth in "Economy," for Thoreau sees these necessities as variations of the one vital necessity of maintaining body heat. The pervasive use of analogies in *Walden*, then, illustrates the same principle of economy through repetition.

Finally, Thoreau's symbolism exploits the paradox of identity-in-difference. Like word plays and analogies, symbols are economical, for Walden Pond is both itself and the locus of many different meanings. Yet the economy of symbolism is more than simply literary. Thoreau is "thankful that this pond was made deep and pure for a symbol" (p. 287), and he regards the whole of nature as material for symbols. Perry Miller writes that for Thoreau "these metaphors—or, as he sometimes called them, 'types'—were the rewards of an exploitation of natural resources, as self-centered, as profit-seeking, as that of any railroad-builder or lumber-baron, as that of any John Jacob Astor."[32] Although we might not like Miller's tone, his statement accurately describes the exploitative economy that underlies Thoreau's symbolism. Symbolism was peculiarly congenial to Thoreau, then, because it was doubly economical: it was both consistent with his formal concern for economy through repetition and served the needs of his imperialism —his trade with nature.

Thoreau's method of composing *Walden* reflects the same concerns that inform his technique. As J. Lyndon Shanley has shown, *Walden* assumed its present form and dimensions only after a long process of accretion, for Thoreau revised his original manuscript seven times. Thus the final version is the contraction of a series of time spans into one form. Not only is the related experience contracted from two years into one, but the book itself represents a condensation of seven or eight years of revisions. An even longer span of time is in question, however, because in *Walden* Thoreau uses journal entries from as far back as April 1839. Shanley's study of the history of paragraphs 13, 14, and 15 in "Spring" nicely displays Thoreau's mosaic method of composition:

> Paragraph 13 (the stirring of new life) depends on a journal entry which Thoreau made at Staten Island on September 29, 1843; paragraph 14 (Walden "melting apace") depends on what he saw and heard and wrote in his journal some ten years later on March 20 and 21 and April 1, 1853. The excitement and beauty of the events of 1843 and 1853 were characteristic of his springs at the pond, and so he used them with paragraph 15 ("the change from storm and winter"), which depends on the evening of March 26, 1846. He was careful to add about the melting of Walden, "But this spring it broke up more steadily, as I have said." "This spring" was in fact the spring of 1847, after the great ice-cutting venture of 1846–47. But the artistic reference is to the spring of the one year that he was re-creating for his reader.[33]

Moreover, the journal entries themselves were not spontaneous transcriptions of what was going on daily in Thoreau's consciousness. Thoreau admits, "I am startled when I consider how little I am *actually* concerned about the things I write in my journal" (*J*, 1:143). When we consider the *Journal* as a whole in the light of this admission, Thoreau's lack of compunction about bringing entries from 1839 and 1854 together in *Walden* becomes more understandable.

Neither the *Journal* nor *Walden* was conceived as a chronological transcription of a process of growth; instead, each seems to deny a linear process of change. Since a number of the "facts" of *Walden* were provided after the experience of Walden, Thoreau's understanding of facts would seem to be nonhistorical. Representing the accretion of a fifteen-year period, then, *Walden* is a transcendence of this span of time. Thoreau knew that "thoughts of different dates will not cohere" (*J*, 3:288), yet it was by making the thoughts "cohere" that he transcended the "different dates." In its method as well as its themes, therefore, *Walden* denies endings. Yet the first paragraph of *Walden* and the final paragraph of "Spring," which respectively introduce and sum up the Walden experiment, insist on the historical nature of the experience. Not only in a structural but in an autobiographical sense, then, there are in fact a beginning and an end in *Walden*. Thoreau undertook the impossible task of writing an autobiographical work denying personal limitations in time and space. Thus *Walden* is personal history transcending itself, because both Thoreau's thematic conversion of naturalistic cycles to Emersonian circles and his method—the very history of *Walden*'s making—constitute a denial of historical time.

The mosaic method is of a piece with the other patterns of resurrection in *Walden*, for it represents the continual resurrection not only of the self at Walden but of earlier and later selves. If in *Walden* Thoreau reconstructed his past, however, he had to some extent already constructed the future. As Perry Miller points out, Thoreau made journal entries in anticipation of certain kinds of experiences and used this material later.[34] Indeed, this idea of anticipating events in life as well as in nature—Thoreau's grand ambition—can be seen as repetition in reverse. "Can I not," he asks, "by expectation affect the revolutions of nature, make a day bring forth something new?" (*J*, 3:438). Whether through recollection or anticipation, then, repetition is the principle that informs Thoreau's method.

Robert Frost has written that "Thoreau's immortality may hang by a single book, but the book includes even his writing that is *not* in it. Nothing he ever said but sounds like a quotation from it. Think of the success of a man's pulling himself together under one one-word title. Enviable."[35] We have seen that Thoreau condensed many years of experience into *Walden*, and, as a result, *Walden* in fact expands to contain the whole person. Thoreau's life and art form a whole, because he was not simply writing his autobiography and recollecting his life in tranquility at a distance from the events. The impulse of his art was autobiographical from its inception; after all, Thoreau started writing by keeping a journal. As a result, his personal writing went beyond recording his life to actually shaping what he should expect and what he would find to record—that is, the art came to create the life.

This development was possible for Thoreau, for the needs of the peculiar man that he chose to remain and the needs of the peculiar artist that he chose to become met and were met in autobiography. As Thoreau practiced it, autobiography offered not only an opportunity for self-cultivation but the possibility of self-creation; not only the pleasures of repetition and resurrection of time past but the ecstasies of the transcendence of history itself; not only a satisfaction of the demands of economy but the extravagance of proliferation; and not only the justification for the self-absorption of narcissism but the chance to recapture the organic wholeness of Narcissus's universe.

Thoreau's life and art come together as a perfect whole, because he both chose a personal art form—the continual recording of the minutiae of daily life—and made his life itself into a source of art. Like Whitman, Thoreau resembles such artists as Baudelaire and Kierkegaard, who made their lives into art by choosing their fate. According to Paul Zweig in *The Heresy of Self-Love*, Kierkegaard and Baudelaire willed themselves to be what they already were.[36] But with the difference, we might add, of self-consciousness, the mode in which their new verbal selves exist.

By deliberately choosing what he already was, then, Thoreau also succeeded in making his life into art and himself into the hero. His attention was never divided: his claim in *Walden* that "we are all sculptors and painters, and our material is our own flesh and blood and bones" (p. 221) recalls his somewhat more graphic journal entry of 1840, "He is the true artist whose life is his material; every stroke of the chisel must enter his own flesh and bone and not grate dully on marble" (J, 1:149). Even Thoreau's so-called political acts—his civil disobedience and the John Brown speech—could be seen as basically aesthetic. By his own admission Thoreau was not interested in politics, and if his *Journal* is any indication, he was largely oblivious to the political news of his day. These acts must be seen, then, in the light of his exquisite and undivided self-contemplation, for even in these public acts it was the "few cubic feet of flesh" that Thoreau was cultivating (p. 5).

Once the hero myth is internalized, the goal becomes an ideal of spiritual purity and perfection that is located inside the hero, and the search turns inward to discover a permanent center. As Zweig suggests, however, the internalization of the hero myth involves a paradox.[37] The hero's ordeal consists of withdrawal into oneself and isolation from society; indeed, Ellery Channing bid Thoreau, "go out upon that [field], build yourself a hut, & there begin the grand process of devouring yourself alive."[38] If the ordeal is to become heroic, however, the hero's quest must be communicated. Once again, then, self-consciousness emerges as a literary mode—in this case, as an awareness of the problematical nature of the reporting. For the poet-hero must be a hermit and a public hero at the same time—simultaneously subjective and objective. Thoreau is aware of this problem when he casts himself as the Representative Man: "If I seem to boast more than is becoming, my excuse is that I brag for humanity rather than for myself; and my shortcomings and inconsistencies do not affect the truth of my statement" (p. 49). In making himself into a mirror or a representative man, Thoreau becomes an objective hero whose heroism consists of his unrelenting subjectivity. Lowell perceived the problematical nature of Thoreau's position when he wrote, "This egotism of his is a Stylites pillar after all, a seclusion which keeps him in the public eye."[39]

In making oneself into a mirror in one's art, the poet-hero escapes to some extent from the egocentricity of self-contemplation by at the same time presenting readers with an image of themselves. *Walden* not only gives Thoreau an identity but becomes *our* mirror—*our* Walden Pond; indeed, Thoreau asks us to measure ourselves by the ideal of purity that is represented there. And the reflection that is *Walden* is no less vital than the experience at Walden: you must "defend your eyes against the reflected as well as the true sun," Thoreau writes, "for they are equally bright; and if, between the two, you survey [Walden's] surface critically, it is literally as smooth as glass" (p. 186). Appropriately, then, the name of the book and the name of the mirror-lake are the same, and Thoreau understandably dropped "Life in the Woods" from the original title.

Just as writing delivered Thoreau from himself, we are delivered from our own egocentricity while reading *Walden*. As Georges Poulet has written, we discover the author's self speaking within us when we read.[40] Thoreau himself shares this view of reading, for he considers a work of literature as the work of art "nearest to life itself" because it must "not only be read but actually breathed from all human lips"—it must be "carved out of the breath of life itself" (p. 102). In the act of reading, then, we transcend our identity and can say, in Thoreau's words, that "it was I in him that was then so bold, and it is he in me that now reviews the vision" (p. 99). Thus reading as well as writing is a narcissistic act, for the process of discovering another within us liberates us from our identity; like Narcissus, we are no longer self-absorbed or cold. If we follow Thoreau's instructions and read *Walden* "as deliberately and reservedly" (p. 101) as it was written, we come to repeat his carefully plotted liberation from identity and, consequently, from time as well. For "we must be born again in order to speak" (p. 101) the language of literature.

As Thoreau suggests, this deliverance from identity is also an escape from time. Indeed, this transcendence of time is central to the artistic experience, and Thoreau's story of the "artist of Kouroo" could be read as a parable of the creation of *Walden* itself. Since "into a perfect work time does not enter," the artist who dedicated himself to perfection "grew not older by a moment. His singleness of purpose and resolution, and his elevated piety, endowed him, without his knowledge, with perennial youth. As he made no compromise with Time, Time kept out of his way" (p. 326). The artist is protected from time because what he creates is self-contained: "He had made a new *system* in making a staff, a world with full and fair proportions" (p. 327, italics mine). Similarly, we can say of a temporal or literary work of art that its time span is a complete life-time. Thus the consciousness that comes into being while reading a book and that is lost at the end lives through a life cycle, and all complete life cycles may be seen to represent equal time spans. The freedom from time, then, extends to the reader as well, for not only Thoreau's two years at Walden and the eight years that he took to write *Walden* but the hours that one takes to *read* it are equivalent to the one complete life cycle that is the subject of the book.

Thoreau writes in "Economy": "Could a greater miracle take place than for us to look through each other's eyes for an instant? We should live in all the ages of the world in an hour; ay, in all the worlds of the ages. History, Poetry, Mythology!—I know of no reading of another's experience so startling and informing as this would be" (p. 10). In "Reading," when he calls for the reader's critical participation, it is this miracle that he hopes to achieve in *Walden*, and his autobiographical form, which is not history, poetry, or mythology but a personal fusion of all three, is designed to offer such a look below the surface. In art, then, time is not mechanical but is transcended, repetition is in fact possible, and the reader as well as the author lives more than one life. In the hours that we take to read *Walden*, we repeat years of Thoreau's life. And herein lies one of the pleasures of literature—its economy.

Chapter 2
"Walt Whitman, a Kosmos,
of Manhattan the Son"

"Song of Myself" is a curious poem: of most of the things that can be said about it, the opposite can also be said. The poem has attracted a number of different, often contradictory readings, yet somehow it stands—like its hero—"apart from the pulling and hauling," "amused, complacent," and "unitary."[1] Thus the poem that is advertised as the most open turns out to be highly self-contained. If we approach "Song of Myself" as autobiography, however, we can account for the kinds of doubleness that riddle it and render it so elusive, for these dualities arise precisely from Whitman's attempt to transcend the dualisms inherent in personal literature.

As we have seen, autobiographical writing necessarily involves a splitting or doubling of the self. In the act of writing about oneself, the author becomes narrator and hero, observer and observed, subject and object, and the two selves are like mirror images of each other; they are the same yet opposites. This doubling or splitting of the self is the source of the self-consciousness that characterizes autobiographical writing. As practiced by Whitman, however, autobiography is a self-transcending mode. Whitman unites the self by defining consciousness—the self as subject—as literal self-consciousness or consciousness of the self as object. Thus it is "touch" that quivers *him* to a "new identity." This maneuver parallels the way in which he transcends the duality of the "Me myself" and "me" of section 4 of "Song of Myself," for in section 5 the body becomes proof of the wholeness or marriage of spirit and the particular "I," since the body is both universal and unique. By defining consciousness as literal self-consciousness, Whitman can remain a time-bound individual and still transcend himself, for now the hero comes to incorporate all that he sees or experiences. In other words, whatever the persona is conscious of, he is necessarily conscious of as part of himself.

Thus the problem of subjectivity that troubled the Romantics never arose for Whitman. Discussing the autobiographical nature of Romantic literature, Robert Langbaum observes that the acceptance of the subjective nature of meaning in the nineteenth century resulted in the poets' feeling trapped in their subjectivity. The cures for this "disease" ranged from locating poems in time and space and casting them as occurrences to assuming stances of avowed insincerity, and poets had finally to hide behind masks in an attempt to conceal the subjective origin of their ideas and to give them objectivity and authority.[2] Consequently, Langbaum sees Browning and Tennyson as bridging Romanticism and Modernism. Seen against this background, Whitman seems curiously removed from the concerns of his contemporaries. He also had to write about himself, but the mask that he chose was one of total and omnivorous subjectivity. As we have seen, "I" is the most subjective yet most universal of persons, and since Whitman makes his "I" more subjective than Thoreau's, he achieves a more complete—indeed, a mythic—universality.

Similarly, the Romantic separation of mind and world is foreign to Whitman in "Song of Myself," where the inner and the outer are not separated. Such dualistic terminology is itself alien to Whitman, and we may consider the sensibility in the poem either as an overgrown subjectivity, which has swallowed up the objective, or even as an overly demanding objectivity, which has shattered the subject into its myriad perceptions. Indeed, the undifferentiated, fluid matrix of the poem may be seen to constitute a mythic universe. According to Ernst Cassirer, in mythic experience the person "reveals reality to himself, and himself to reality, in that he lets himself and the environment enter into this plastic medium, in which the two do not merely make contact, but fuse with each other." And at the moment that the subject and object fuse—at the moment, that is, of initial perception—a sound is uttered spontaneously, and subject and object flow into each other. Thus language arises from and objectifies the subject's inner excitement in the face of the object, and the uttering of the word relieves the tension: "The conscious experience is not merely wedded to the word, but is consumed by it. Whatever has been fixed by a name, henceforth is not only real, but is Reality. . . . in place of a more or less adequate 'expression,' we find a relation of identity, of complete congruence between 'image' and 'object,' between the name and the thing." Significantly, Cassirer sees poetry as the one activity that preserves and continually renews the original creative power of the word.[3] The creation of this kind of mythic universe in "Song of Myself" represents a return to the beginnings of human consciousness, when language, myth, and art sprang from the same matrix in the same act of self-discovery before the world. Whitman's extravagant claim for his poem—"Stop this day and night with me and you shall possess the origin of all poems" (sec. 2)—should be read in this context.

Yet Whitman's creation of a mythic universe, which enabled him to transcend the subject-object dualism inherent in autobiography, involved him in another duality, for the undifferentiated, mythic universe of the persona was in conflict with the necessarily historical universe of autobiographical writing. This tension between myth and history may characterize autobiographical literature in general, for the inclusiveness of consciousness—the universal "I"—as hero militates against the historical individuation of the author in autobiography. In Whitman, this tension is heightened, because his very project embodied a conflict between myth and history. Whitman intended in "Song of Myself" to present a mythic hero and also to create an American hero out of himself and his historical environment. Thus the figure "Walt Whitman" represents a culture hero, which is neither the purely human hero of the folk tale nor the full-fledged divinity of myth but, in Susanne Langer's terms, a "hybrid." Although part god, the culture hero acts in this world, and these actions affect real people forever after; the culture hero has, therefore, "a somewhat vague, yet unmistakable historical relation to living men, and a tie to the locality on which he has left his mark."[4]

Whitman created this culture hero in the first person and in his own image; indeed, perhaps the American hero had to be an "I." In any case, Whitman's project involved him in and, at the same time, detached him from his cultural and historical environment. He was "both in and out" of this game: while the "I" was universal as a biological being and cosmic—or in the image of God—as consciousness, as personality it was historically bound. The "Me myself" or "what I am" stands both in and out of history, "watching and wondering" at the "game"—"Battles, the horrors of fratricidal war, the fever of doubtful news, the fitful events" (sec. 4). The hero, then, is a "kosmos" *and* "of Manhattan the son" (sec. 24), and his "song" is accordingly timeless yet enmeshed in its time.

"Song of Myself" may be called mythic autobiography, because the consciousness that evolves within the poem is an ahistorical, mythic consciousness. If this consciousness is outside historical time, however, as a "kosmos" and as biological being it is also the very source of the concept of time. Moreover, in the mythic universe of "Song of Myself," the biological and cosmic cycles are analogous not only to each other but to the cycles of consciousness. It is in fact through analogies between the biological and the cosmic that the mythic consciousness apprehends itself and the world. In Cassirer's words:

> . . . for mythical consciousness and feeling a kind of biological time, a rhythmic ebb and flow of life, precedes the intuition of a properly cosmic time. Actually, cosmic time itself is first apprehended by myth in this peculiar biological form, for to the mythical consciousness the regularity of the natural process, the periodicity of the planets and the seasons, appears entirely as a life process. At first the mythical consciousness apprehends the change of day into night, the flowering and fading of plants, and the cyclical order of the seasons only by projecting these phenomena into human existence, where it perceives them as in a mirror.[5]

It is the rhythm of breathing—the inflow and outflow of

spirit or life—that constitutes the underlying biological pattern of the characteristic movements of "Song of Myself."

If we compare "Song of Myself" with a Romantic autobiographical poem like Wordsworth's *The Prelude*, we see how in Whitman the poetic remains surprisingly biological. Both Wordsworth and Whitman begin with the conventional Romantic invocation of the wind as the source of poetic inspiration. In Wordsworth, the "gentle breeze" blesses him and stirs a "correspondent breeze" within him. The wind or "spirit" that animates nature awakens Wordsworth's spirit and thereby provides his poetic inspiration. Like Wordsworth, Whitman invokes the "atmosphere" as his inspiration:

> It is for my mouth forever, I am in love with it,
>
> · · · · · · · · · · · ·
>
> I am mad for it to be in contact with me. (Sec. 2)

In Whitman, however, the "correspondent breeze" is not a metaphor for spirit but is breath itself:

> My respiration and inspiration, the beating of my heart,
>   the passing of blood and air through my lungs,
>
> · · · · · · · · · · · ·
>
> The sound of the belch'd words of my voice loos'd to the
>   eddies of the wind, (Sec. 2)

Whitman's inspiration is quite literally his "inspiration," and as the outer air or atmosphere becomes inner air or breath, his song of himself becomes at the same time a song of the world. Thus breathing—the biological amalgamation or filtering of air by the tissues—is the process in which the world and the self fuse. Through this radical identification of body and spirit, world and self, Whitman transports himself from a biological to a mythic universe.

Whitman not only equates breathing with poetic inspiration but models his account of poetic creation after "respiration and inspiration." "Partaker of influx and efflux" (sec.

22), the poet absorbs the scenes, people, and objects around him and sends them back out again transformed, as the air is transformed in the process of breathing:

> Dazzling and tremendous how quick the sun-rise would kill me,
> If I could not now and always send sun-rise out of me.
> (Sec. 25)

Accordingly, the catalog in section 15 concludes:

> And these tend inward to me, and I tend outward to them,
> And such as it is to be of these more or less I am,
> And of these one and all I weave the song of myself.

And in section 19 Whitman writes of his poem:

> This the far-off depth and height reflecting my own face,
> This the thoughtful merge of myself, and the outlet again.

The reader is to repeat the poet's act of creation: "You shall listen to all sides," Whitman writes, "and filter them from your self" (sec. 2). "Filter" recalls "the passing of blood and air through my lungs" and returns us once again to the process of breathing that is central to the poem. This theme culminates in section 52, when the persona vanishes into thin air:

> I depart as air, I shake my white locks at the runaway sun,
> I effuse my flesh in eddies, and drift it in lacy jags.
> . . . .
> You will hardly know who I am or what I mean,
> But I shall be good health to you nevertheless,
> And filter and fibre your blood.

We are meant, then, to inhale Whitman, for he would be our inspiration. The cannibalistic role in which the reader is cast reflects the poet's own cannibalism: "All this I swallow," he writes, "it tastes good, I like it well, it becomes mine" (sec. 33). Characteristically, Whitman's literalness performs double duty, and he can write of his poem:

> This is the meal equally set, this the meat for natural hunger,
> It is for the wicked just the same as the righteous . . .
> (Sec. 19)

Thus reading would be an act of communion—physical *and* spiritual.

Even the rhythm of Whitman's line, which reenacts the primary movement of breath, evinces the biologically autobiographical nature of "Song of Myself." F. O. Matthiessen claims that "Whitman's desire to give up borrowed cadences altogether came from his crude re-living of the primitive evolution of poetry" and observes that Whitman's rhythms respond not only to bodily movements and activities but to the "internal pulsations of the body."[6] Whitman's rhythm corresponds to the rhythm of breathing, for each line is uttered as an independent unit that at the same time is part of a pattern of repetitions. Because his lines usually break in the middle, each line may also be said to dilate and contract; for example, lines like "I celebrate myself, and sing myself," "My faith is the greatest of faiths, and the least of faiths," and "Not words of routine this song of mine" exhibit this pattern of dilation and contraction. Breaking his lines in the middle also enabled Whitman to link the abstract statement with the concrete: "I concentrate toward them that are nigh, I wait on the door-slab." As this line exemplifies, and as F. O. Matthiessen and John Lynen note, Whitman frequently juxtaposes an expansive, bardic style and a simpler, more colloquial manner in the same line.[7]

The movement of dilation and contraction or inflow and outflow informs much of the imagery of the poem as well. The images of evolution, for example, reflect this movement: "I am an acme of things accomplish'd, and I am encloser of things to be" (sec. 44). Similarly, the astronomical and sea imagery may be seen as cosmic mirrorings of biological patterns. "Backing and filling, appearing and disappearing," Whitman identifies both with the moon "carrying the crescent child that carries its own full mother in its belly" (sec. 33) and with the sea "breathing broad and convulsive breaths": "I am integral with you," he writes, "I too am of one phase and of all phases" (sec. 22). Whitman's image of writing as translating is yet another reflection of this in-and-out movement. If for Emerson the poet is "representative of man, in virtue of being the largest power to receive and to impart," for Whitman also writing is the process of simultaneously receiving and imparting or, in Gertrude Stein's terms, "at the same time telling and listening to anything or everything."[8] Consequently, writing becomes a kind of translating; for instance, Whitman wants to "translate" the "uniform hieroglyphic" and the "so many uttering tongues" (sec. 6) of the grass in order to solve the mystery of being for which the grass stands. Likewise, Whitman's imagery equates poetic and sexual creation, because the rhythms of procreation are analogous to the rhythm of breath. This recurrent pattern of dilation and contraction in Whitman seems to have sprung from the rhythms of his life, and in this sense it is truly auto-biographical. Roger Asselineau sees Whitman's life as alternating periods of crisis and subsequent release through poetic creation. Following Asselineau, R. W. B. Lewis in fact divides Whitman's life into phases of going out and coming in: periods of waiting, absorbing, and listening are countered by periods of inspiration and activity.[9]

Analogous to the basic movement of inspiration and respiration is the vacillation of the Whitman persona between birth and death. Kenneth Burke, for example, observes that Whitman is continually going "out of the cradle" and into the arms of the "death" that the sea whispers to him.[10] Thus the active, emerging "male" force in Whitman is opposed by the "female" death principle, and this opposition informs the movements of the persona not only within sections but in the entire poem, from the an-

nouncement of the birth of a poet to his death and projected dissolution. For in the end the persona becomes the
earth and nourishment for the leaves of grass. The assertions of life in Whitman, then, are balanced by the claims
of death which, in turn, holds a promise of rebirth, and
this death wish explains the desire of the Whitman persona
continually to merge with other people or the landscape.

A cycle at once biological and cosmic informs even the
structure of "Song of Myself." The "I" as biological being
is, in a sense, itself "the clock," for its very rhythms keep
time, while it stands outside historical time. Accordingly,
whereas the experience in "Song of Myself" tends—as we
shall see—toward a triumphant transcendence of space
and time, the poem is peculiarly enmeshed in time and
space. For example, section 33, in which the persona finally
transcends space and time and is "afoot" with his "vision,"
also locates the persona's experience in space and time:

> Space and Time! now I see it is true, what I guess'd at,
> What I guess'd when I loaf'd on the grass, [See secs.
>   1–17]
> What I guess'd while I lay alone in my bed, [Possibly
>   secs. 21, 27, and 28]
> And again as I walk'd the beach under the paling
>   stars of the morning. [See secs. 22–25]

The transcendence of time both proceeds in temporal stages
and occurs within the context of objective time. The poem
encompasses one day, from the "transparent summer
morning" that recalls another such morning in section 5
to the setting of the sun in section 52: "The last scud of
day holds back for me." And "the song of me rising from
bed and meeting the sun" (sec. 2) concludes with the
persona departing like the "runaway sun." The poem also
observes the unity of place, for the persona starts out on,
keeps returning to, and finally ends up as the grass: "If
you want me again look for me under your boot-soles" (sec.
52). Thus the cycle of consciousness that *is* the poem—
that comes into being as the poem and is destroyed with

the end of it—is analogous to the biological cycles of inspiration and expiration, of life and death. Likewise, there
are cosmic analogies of these cycles in the waxing and
waning of the moon, in the ebb and flow of the tides, and
ultimately in the rising and setting of the sun.

Whitman's "I" becomes universal not only by remaining
fundamentally biological but by assuming mythic proportions, and as a result "Song of Myself" avoids the particularity of most autobiographical writing. Remaining biological, the hero's objectivity is his very subjectivity—the
"smoke" of his breath is his poetic inspiration. Assuming
the dimensions of a "kosmos," however, his subjectivity
itself becomes objective, for now the "I" speaks with the
voice of Being itself. Indeed, Nietzsche defines the lyric "I"
as the cosmos speaking through the similitude of one person.[11] Depending upon how we approach it, then, "Song of
Myself" is either biological autobiography or mythic autobiography. In any case, the hero has neither privacy nor a
historically definable objective existence, for in his universe
there is no distinction between the subjective and the objective.

Whether we approach "Song of Myself" as biological or
as mythic autobiography, the wholeness that its hero
achieves results from his embracing both sides of various
sets of opposites. The mythic "I" or "I" as consciousness is
a whole that encompasses opposites and thus approximates
Jung's psychological archetype of the self. According to
Jung, it is the figure of Christ that in the West has symbolized the archetypal self: "As an historical personage
Christ is unitemporal and unique; as God, universal and
eternal. Likewise the self: as an individual thing it is unitemporal and unique; as an archetypal symbol it is a God-
image and therefore universal and eternal." The psychological archetype has light and dark aspects as well,
for it contains both good and evil, which in Christian
symbolism become Christ and Antichrist. Likewise, the

archetypal self has masculine and feminine aspects and is symbolized as the marriage of opposites. Jung explains the characteristic dualities of the self-symbol in psychological not metaphysical terms: the act of cognition itself must posit or create oppositions that will make discrimination possible.[12]

The Whitman persona in fact contains the dualities that Jung attributes to the self-archetype: he is unitemporal and eternal, unique and universal, good and evil, masculine and feminine. The poet who writes,

> One's-self I sing, a simple separate person,
> Yet utter the word Democratic, the word En-Masse,[13]

is at the same time "the poet of the Body" and "the poet of the Soul" (sec. 21), "the poet of the woman the same as the man" (sec. 21), and "the poet of goodness" and "the poet of wickedness also" (sec. 22). He announces,

> I am of old and young, of the foolish as much as the wise,
> Regardless of others, ever regardful of others,
> Maternal as well as paternal, a child as well as a man,
> (Sec. 16)

and proceeds to become even more daring:

> What blurt is this about virtue and about vice?
> Evil propels me and reform of evil propels me, I stand indifferent, (Sec. 22)

The poet makes good his claims by assuming vastly different identities; he becomes at once female and male, good and evil, human and godlike.

A number of critics have emphasized Whitman's inclusiveness. F. O. Matthiessen, for example, characterizes this inclusiveness as "regressive, infantile fluidity." Accordingly, Edwin Miller and Quentin Anderson see Whitman's universe as the universe of the polymorphous perverse, in which the persona rejects the differentiation of sexual roles.[14] This psychological approach fails, however, to account for all Whitman's dualisms, for in Whitman it is not only the sexual that remains fluid and undefined. Truer to Whitman's expansiveness is Randall Jarrell's statement that Whitman "says over and over that there are in him good and bad, wise and foolish, anything at all and its antonym, and he is telling the truth; there is in him almost everything in the world, so that one responds to him, willingly or unwillingly, almost as one does to the world."[15] Seeing "Song of Myself" as the creation of an archetypal or mythic self enables us to account for the wide range of oppositions in Whitman.

Thus Whitman's statement that *Leaves of Grass* should not be considered as a "poem mainly" becomes understandable,[16] for he intended—in "Song of Myself," at least—to create a self-archetype for America. And his description of *Leaves of Grass* as "a language experiment" is not inconsistent with this intention: the new hero had, after all, to speak a new, even primitive, language. In a pertinent article on the antithetical meaning of "primal words," Freud quotes from Karl Abel's discussion of ancient Egyptian: "Now in the Egyptian language, this unique relic of a primitive world, we find a fair number of words with two meanings, one of which says the exact opposite of the other. Imagine, if one can imagine anything so obviously nonsensical, that the word 'strong' in German means 'weak' as well as 'strong' . . ." Since cognition itself arises from comparisons and oppositions, words with antithetical meanings would seem to be common to all languages in their primitive stages, and Freud cites some examples from German and English: "To our *bös* (bad) corresponds a *bass* (good); in Old Saxon compare *bat* (good) with English *bad* . . ."[17] Similarly, certain words in Whitman come to include their opposites and thereby regain this original, psychologically basic comprehensiveness. Life and death, for example, become identified; opposites, they constitute a whole. Life comes also to mean death, and death, life:

And as to you Corpse I think you are good manure,
    but that does not offend me,
I smell the white roses sweet-scented and growing,

.   .   .   .

And as to you Life I reckon you are the leavings of many
    deaths, (Sec. 49)

In the same way, the "I" contains multitudes, while the many cohere as one; the past and the future, here and everywhere, and now and always are likewise seen as opposites that include each other.

As opposites blend into each other, even moral distinctions disappear, and morality in "Song of Myself" comes down to "sympathy," which ideally does not distinguish between the good and the evil or the innocent and the wicked. Although D. H. Lawrence has denounced Whitman's refusal to make moral distinctions,[18] such inclusiveness is part of the project that Whitman undertook in "Song of Myself": just as the persona himself is both good and evil, so too is his universe, and his sympathies must be correspondingly large. Whitman's persona is universal, then, because he is complete or whole, and he is whole because his very nature is division. Embracing both parts of a duality, the "I" becomes whole.

As biological being and as mythic archetype, Whitman's persona is whole, and his universe is accordingly undivided. If the subjective and objective remain undifferentiated, however, autobiography in the usual sense becomes impossible, since an undivided universe precludes a historical perspective. Thus we find in Whitman not a narrative of events arranged on a continuum of temporal causality but a mimesis of direct perception immersed in time. Since in Whitman there is no distinction between the subjective and objective realms, the observing self cannot be static or detached from time; the historical causality of a narrative, therefore, is out of the question.

Another comparison of "Song of Myself" with *The Pre-*

lude reveals how Whitman's vision of an undifferentiated universe precluded a narrative structure. For example, Wordsworth sees the childhood incident of the stolen boat as the causal antecedent of his mature understanding of nature. Yet we could reverse Wordsworth's order and argue that his understanding of nature at the time of the writing causes the incident to become a symbolic event. Although events may not have been related by temporal causality, they are arranged causally in retrospect. This arrangement is possible because the narrative situation is stationary: the observer pretends to be static in time and assumes a fixed point of view. If the narrative situation were continually shifting, however, the point of view would also change, and the result would be a multiple exposure of causal sequences of the kind that we in fact find in "Song of Myself." Since the perception of a causal pattern is contingent upon the persona's detachment from the primary experience, a point of view that coincides in time with the experience of the poem cannot arrange events as a narrative—that is, as a temporal, causal sequence.

And because Whitman's narrative situation remains fluid, "Song of Myself" cannot be considered a narrative or a recording of an experience. The poem begins with the claims of what might be a particularly aggressive poet:

I celebrate myself, and sing myself,
And what I assume you shall assume, (Sec. 1)

The persona becomes more particular and at the same time explicitly universal when he identifies himself as

Walt Whitman, a kosmos, of Manhattan the son,
Turbulent, fleshy, sensual, eating, drinking and breeding. (Sec. 24)

In the series of identifications in section 33, the persona becomes even more particularized while, paradoxically, asserting his universality: "I am the man, I suffer'd, I was there." In section 41 the persona comes to assume "the exact dimensions of Jehovah" and proceeds to enlarge until he incorporates all creation. Continually changing, he remains "untranslatable," and his warning stands: "Encompass worlds, but never try to encompass me" (sec. 25). Since a continually changing speaker precludes a particular narrative order, then, "Song of Myself" cannot be considered an epic,[19] even though it is a mimesis of direct address.

In the absence of a narrative order, the concept of repetition enables us to account for the structure of "Song of Myself," for the poem repeats from different points of view a basic process of absorption. If a poet is speaking, he registers all that he sees, hears, and experiences, as in section 15; if a "kosmos" is speaking, however, he catalogs all that he includes. And if the persona is godlike or free of space, time, and identity, then he lists all that he is, as in section 33. Finally, if he becomes identified with the earth itself, he can speak even of what will be. Although John Lynen notes Whitman's repetitiveness, he interprets it as a way of maintaining an unchanging "now" throughout the poem.[20] As the life processes themselves illustrate, however, repetition through time is change, and this change is not simply quantitative but qualitative as well. Thus Lynen's interpretation reveals the same lack of a temporal-historical viewpoint that he proposes to study in Whitman, for the poem is no more a static juxtaposition of a series of "nows" than it is a narrative progression. Since "Song of Myself" is not only myth but autobiography, the unchanging now of a mythic universe would be as inappropriate to the poem as the temporal causality of historical narrative.

Instead, "Song of Myself" exhibits the compromise of an evolutionary order. Although an evolutionary progression is not uniform but repetitive and subject to setbacks and reversals, it is nevertheless a historical and ultimately irreversible process. Yet it differs from the progression of historical narrative, because evolutionary events are linked on the basis of structural affinity, not by explicit, linear causality. Thus "Song of Myself" unfolds in many directions at once. As we proceed through the poem, and especially as we approach the middle, echoes and repetitions of preceding sections begin to build up so densely that in the process of going forward we keep returning to earlier lines. Affirming the immanence of God in section 48, for example, Whitman writes, "I find letters from God dropt in the street, and every one is sign'd by God's name." Yet this line recalls section 32, where Whitman uses the same image to express his evolutionary affinity with animals:

So they show their relations to me and I accept them,
They bring me tokens of myself . . .

I wonder where they get those tokens,
Did I pass that way huge times ago and negligently
    drop them?

Whitman's subsequent reference to these tokens as "remembrancers" returns us to section 6, where the image is first used to describe the grass:

Or I guess it is the handkerchief of the Lord,
A scented gift and remembrancer designedly dropt,

Another example of the growth of significance through repetition is Whitman's treatment of the idea of endless progress. In section 45 Whitman says of "the far-sprinkled systems" that

Wider and wider they spread, expanding, always
    expanding,
Outward and outward and forever outward.
  .   .   .   .
There is no stoppage and never can be stoppage.

This passage reminds us of his earlier, Emersonian use of the image of expanding circles: "All goes onward and outward, nothing collapses" (sec. 6). By echoing the earlier line, the facts of astronomy take on spiritual significance, and at the same time the idea of eternity comes to be supported by the facts. Moreover, through sheer repetition, Whitman enmeshes the reader in a network of images of waiting and inviting, tongues and translation, and doors and compasses. The poem becomes an exercise in field perception, and its structure reinforces the persona's claim that he is in all places at all times. Describing the massacred soldiers (sec. 34), for instance, Whitman employs the very words that he uses in earlier sections to describe himself, and in this way he substantiates his claim that he too was "there" and "suffer'd." In "Song of Myself," then, the past gains in significance as it is continually reborn in the present, and the present likewise grows in meaning as it embodies the past.

In the evolutionary progression of "Song of Myself," each section is included in or absorbed by subsequent sections, and the persona's claim to be "an acme of things accomplish'd" and an "encloser of things to be" (sec. 44)—which is valid in terms of evolution—could stand to characterize each stage of the poem. For although each part is largely independent, it incorporates in abbreviated form what led up to it, much as ontogeny recapitulates phylogeny. Thus not only the progress of the poem but the progress of the persona within the poem—whether from "fetid carbon" to man or from poet to deity—should be seen as an ascension:

> My feet strike an apex of the apices of the stairs,
> On every step bunches of ages, and larger bunches
>   between the steps,
> All below duly travel'd, and still I mount and mount.
>   (Sec. 44)

And the persona's ascent places phenomena in a new light:

> I ascend from the moon, I ascend from the night,
> I perceive that the ghastly glimmer is noonday
>   sunbeams reflected, (Sec. 49)

As the persona ascends, his point of view changes, and his correspondingly enlarging vista encompasses all the stages of his progress.

The evolutionary idea of progress through repetition or recapitulation serves as a model both for the form and meaning of "Song of Myself" and for Whitman's style. In one of the most perceptive discussions of Whitman's style, Basil de Selincourt observes that in Whitman's lines repetition of substance replaces the metrical repetition of pattern. Whereas meter is transitionary and serves to carry the reader smoothly from one line to another, Whitman's kind of repetition renders each line more or less independent and terminal. According to de Selincourt, "Tyrannous spontaneity allows the poet so little respite that every line must, as it were, contain his personality in the germ." There are no transitional lines in Whitman; each line stands as an independent unit that comes to us in a separate breath and therefore ends with some kind of punctuation.[21] It is by repeating words or phrases, then, that Whitman achieves continuity between lines. In his study of biblical analogies for Whitman's prosody, Gay Wilson Allen also shows that Whitman employs various kinds of parallelisms and that his lines progress through the repetition of thoughts, words, or structures.[22] Thus the use of repetition, which allows Whitman's lines to be independent yet continuous, relates his style to his form, for his sections similarly progress not in terms of temporal or causal relationships but through formal or structural affinities.

The biological and, by reflection, mythic autobiography that Whitman wrote is only one aspect of "Song of Myself." For the poem is, in a sense, two different autobiographies, one superimposed on the other. To begin with, the autobiography that is "Song of Myself" creates "Walt Whitman," the poet-hero of the poem. Although this hero starts out somewhat defined as an individual person in the semi-autobiographical opening lines, he evolves in the course of the poem until finally he transcends all personal limitations and encompasses even time and space. Thus the normal autobiographical order is reversed. Instead of charting the development of a life from pure possibility to the emergence of a particular person who is the result of many conscious choices through time, the poem begins with a

relatively particularized poet and ends with pure possibility. Nevertheless, "Song of Myself" is autobiographical, because it fashions a hero out of, and in the image of, its
poet.

Superimposed upon this development is another autobiography, which is embodied in the historical evolution of
the poem in the course of successive revisions between
1855 and 1892. A tension exists between the movement of
the poem and its history. Whereas the poem moves away
from an individual person toward the undifferentiated universe of myth, we witness in the process of revision a movement away from a free and self-contained mythic universe
toward historical particularization. A comparison of the
1855 and 1892 versions of the opening section of "Song of
Myself" illustrates the historical movement of the poem:

1855

I CELEBRATE MYSELF,
And what I assume you shall assume,
For every atom belonging to me as good belongs to you.

I loafe and invite my soul,
I lean and loafe at my ease . . . observing a spear of
summer grass.

1892

I celebrate myself, and sing myself,
And what I assume you shall assume,
For every atom belonging to me as good belongs to you.

I loafe and invite my soul,
I lean and loafe at my ease observing a spear of summer
grass.

My tongue, every atom of my blood, form'd from this
soil, this air,
Born here of parents born here from parents the same,
and their parents the same,

> I, now thirty-seven years old in perfect health begin,
> Hoping to cease not till death.

> Creeds and schools in abeyance,
> Retiring back a while sufficed at what they are, but never
>   forgotten,
> I harbor for good or bad, I permit to speak at every
>   hazard,
> Nature without check with original energy.

The attribution of the sea "yarn" in section 35 to "my grandmother's father" is another example of how the addition of autobiographical lines after 1855 serves to particularize the hero. Thus, whereas the "I" becomes generalized between sections 1 and 52, between 1855 and 1892 it becomes increasingly particularized.

As Whitman revises "Song of Myself" after 1855, then, the poem moves away from the wholeness of an undifferentiated, mythic universe to the historical world of autobiography. Since the addition of not only personal or autobiographical but also historical details like the allusions to the "fratricidal war" tends to place the poem in a historical setting, its hero becomes correspondingly less transcendent and more a part of a human, social environment. Whitman's revisions also serve the purpose of differentiation: the poem is named, divided into numbered sections, punctuated conventionally, and—with the aid of parenthetical subordination—more consciously structured. Like the evolution of *Leaves of Grass* itself, the history of differentiation that shaped "Song of Myself" represents a process of birth or emergence out of a cosmos. If Thoreau's *Walden* was a personal remembrance that through revision became art, "Song of Myself" was art that through revision became personal.

In psychological interpretations of Whitman, however, his poetry is seen as personal from the beginning. According to de Selincourt's study, for example, the poetry represents the release or expurgation of the double and its passions. Similarly, Edwin Miller emphasizes the personal and sexual basis of the poems.[23] A large number of Whitman's critics, in fact, view the Walt Whitman of the poems as a mask through which Walter Whitman exorcised his personal demons. Following Nietzsche, however, we can turn the psychological interpretation on its head and say that a poem is written not by a particular person but by a poet speaking with the voice of Being itself. Thus it is the universal—the poet Walt Whitman—that speaks through the mask of a particular person, whose problems thereby become only exempla. Poetry, then, does not reveal the nonpoetic but is revealed through the agency of the nonpoetic or the particular person.

Moreover, by gradually making himself into the Walt Whitman of the poetry, Whitman more or less willed "Song of Myself" to become autobiographical in a more conventional sense. "Song of Myself" may be called an autobiography in reverse, for it anticipates a person, and as Asselineau has shown, Whitman evolved in the image of his poem.[24] While in the course of the revisions the hero of the 1855 version became more closely identified with a particular person, Whitman himself patterned his life after the self-image that had been created in 1855. As in the case of Thoreau, life came to imitate art, for Whitman—like Thoreau—considered life to be an aesthetic proposition. The person who became "Walt Whitman" had also been a Broadway dandy and, as Allen has pointed out, was particularly sensitive to the symbolic possibilities of his various occupations even before 1855.[25]

As Whitman changed between 1855 and 1892, however, his self-image also changed. As a result, the history of "Song of Myself" becomes even more complicated, for the poet whom the 1855 version announces is not revising the poem; instead, it is a more self-conscious, public persona who makes the revisions. The expurgations, for example, alter Whitman's self-image, because they are the work of a more conventional poet. More than a public figure, the poet of the revisions is also a self-conscious artist. The 1855 version, as Malcolm Cowley remarks, lacks self-consciousness: "celebrating" himself, the poet of 1855 speaks "compulsively"—he does not "sing."[26] The original "Song of Myself" is a self-contained whole, for it introduces a particular kind of poet, who alone could have written this kind of poetry.

Through the revisions, an alien, artistic self-consciousness enters the self-contained world of the 1855 version. When Whitman comes to refer to his poem or "song" within the poem itself, he betrays a new self-consciousness and a detachment from the poem, and the revised "Song of Myself" is no longer the spontaneous utterance of 1855. For example, Whitman revises

> I think I will do nothing for a long time but listen,
> And accrue what I hear unto myself . . . and let sounds
>   contribute toward me.

to read

> Now I will do nothing but listen,
> To accrue what I hear into this song, to let sounds con-
>   tribute toward it. (Sec. 26)

The poet's separation of himself from his song is seen also in the addition of these lines:

> Absorbing all to myself and for this song. (Sec. 13)

> And of these one and all I weave the song of myself.
>   (Sec. 15)

> Not words of routine this song of mine,
> But abruptly to question, to leap beyond yet nearer bring;
>   (Sec. 42)

This distinction does not mean, however, that there is less artifice in the 1855 version than in the 1892 edition, since the impression of artlessness and spontaneity is achieved through stylistic innovation. "The art of art," Whitman writes in the Preface of 1855, "the glory of expression and the sunshine of the light of letters, is simplicity." And by simplicity Whitman means an artful naturalness: "But to

speak in literature with the perfect rectitude and insouci-
ance of the movements of animals, and the unimpeach-
ableness of the sentiment of trees in the woods and grass
by the roadside, is the flawless triumph of art."[27]

Thus perhaps sincerity in literature is simply the appro-
priateness of the artifice to the purposes for which it is
used. As a self-contained whole, the 1855 version of "Song
of Myself" enjoys this peculiar aptness of artifice. But autobiography is a curious mode, because the hero is also an
artist. If "Song of Myself" presents a spontaneous personality or nature speaking "without check with original energy," it also—as art—formalizes and thereby delimits or
fixes the personality. The very words that reveal the personality as spontaneous and natural serve at the same time
to belie the spontaneity and naturalness of the poet-hero.
According to Jean Starobinski, style in autobiography "takes
on an importance which is not limited to the introduction
of language alone, to the technical search for effects alone:
it becomes 'self-referential,' it undertakes to refer back to
the 'internal' truth within the author."[28] Autobiography,
then, embodies a reflexive movement. The hero—especially
when intended to exemplify a narcissistic lack of self-
consciousness—is plagued by a "double" or style, for the
style and form through which alone the hero can exist paradoxically render this existence inauthentic. The act of revising a poem that originally posed as autochthonic reveals
this paradox inherent in autobiographical art. The revisions, which reveal "Song of Myself" as artifice, militate
against the impression of uniqueness and necessity that the
persona tries to create for his utterances. Moreover, Whitman's returning to "Song of Myself" and worrying, say,
about its punctuation undermines the more grandiose
claims of the persona, which are based precisely on his
being more a prophet than a poet.

"Song of Myself" is riddled with contradictions because
it is autobiographical and, at the same time, recapitulates
a mythic universe in its creation of an archetypal self. Al-

though autobiography can come to assume mythic dimensions due to the universality of the "I," in its style and form it is necessarily individualized and rooted in a particular person and age. Thus what Whitman later wrote about *Leaves of Grass* aptly describes "Song of Myself." Echoing Rousseau's claims for unprecedented frankness, Whitman writes: "This was a feeling or ambition to articulate and faithfully express in literary or poetic form, and uncompromisingly, my own physical, emotional, moral, intellectual, and aesthetic Personality, in the midst of, and tallying, the momentous spirit and facts of its immediate days, and of current America—and to exploit that Personality, identified with place and date, in a far more candid and comprehensive sense than any hitherto poem or book."[29] Whitman's recollected purpose accounts not only for the conflict in his work between sincerity and art but for the tension between a total "Personality," which as a totality becomes archetypal and mythic, and a particular, historical person. As *Leaves of Grass* evolved between 1855 and 1892, and as "Song of Myself" itself changed, Whitman's emphasis shifted from the mythic to the historical. As we have seen, through revision "Song of Myself" became more properly autobiographical and more specifically located in its time.

Yet the historical context was important for Whitman's career from the beginning. Malcolm Cowley and John Kinnaird maintain that the 1855 version of "Song of Myself" lacks a specific historical-political context, which is provided only by the Preface of 1855.[30] Thus the democratic ideology of the Preface would seem to be simply a rhetorical device for making a revolutionary poetry acceptable. According to the chronology of Allen's biography, however, Whitman's ideology went into the making of the poetry, for between 1847 and 1855 he was absorbing and transforming such political ideas. Similarly, Asselineau assigns political causes to the crises that immediately shaped the poetry.[31] We could even say that Whitman's mythic purposes *demanded* a historical context. For the self-symbol to be archetypal, it must be not only timeless but, in fact, temporal: the myth must erupt into history. Thus the age and Whitman's relation to it—his political beliefs, his newspaper career, the political rhetoric that even he was dealing out, his nativism, his imperialism—became part of his song.

The political ideology of the age figured at least in Whitman's conscious designs for his poetry, for he projected a national literature. "A national literature," he knew, "is, of course, in one sense, a great mirror or reflector." Yet he also knew that "there must however be something before —something to reflect."[32] The difficulty was that in America that "something" had never been a given. Consequently, as Perry Miller has observed, Whitman had to keep revising his work, for the subject of his national literature was not a given national myth acting itself out in history but accumulated historical facts—the "statistical survey of the decisions so far made"—trying to shape themselves into a current mythology.[33] By casting his national literature as an extended autobiography, Whitman was able to synthesize history and myth. His poetry not only mythicized history in the crucial formative period of American nationalism but historicized myth, for it re-created a mythic universe and an archetypal self in the very terms of nineteenth-century American history, politics, and language.

Just as the historical context no doubt informed the poetry, the poetry itself helps shape our understanding of the historical period. According to Georg Misch, autobiography offers us "the contemporary intellectual outlook revealed in the style of an eminent person who has himself played a part in the forming of the spirit of his time."[34] One of the reasons, then, that the mid-nineteenth century was the formative period of American nationalism is that it produced a national poet. Thus we look back on this period partly through Whitman; in Jorge Luis Borges's words, Whitman "was also the one he would be in the future, in our future nostalgia, which is created by these prophecies that announced it."[35] In "To a Historian" Whitman claims precisely this role for himself:

> You who celebrate bygones,
> Who have explored the outward, the surfaces of the races, the life that has exhibited itself,
> Who have treated of man as the creature of politics, aggregates, rulers and priests,
> I, habitan of the Alleghanies, treating of him as he is in himself in his own rights,
> Pressing the pulse of the life that has seldom exhibited itself, (the great pride of man in himself,)
> Chanter of Personality, outlining what is yet to be,
> I project the history of the future.[36]

As autobiography, then, "Song of Myself" tends to equate the mythic and the historical. The poem is ahistorical because it embodies a timeless, mythic consciousness, creates an archetypal self, and mythicizes its historical context. Whitman himself insists, however, that his poetry is at the same time historical, for it is rooted in, is informed by, and informs its time. In fact, Whitman saw the poet as mediating between time and eternity: "If [the poet] does not flood himself with the immediate age as with vast oceanic tides—if he be not himself the age transfigur'd, and if to him is not open'd the eternity which gives similitude to all periods and locations and processes, and animate and inanimate forms, and which is the bond of time . . . let him merge in the general run, and wait his development."[37] While Whitman imparted the dignity of a mythic archetype to the historical type of the democratic individual who was not a part but a microcosm of the whole, it was finally through history that this historical type came to assume mythic dimensions. Whitman understood the evolutionary nature of poetry: "No really great song," he claims, "can ever attain full purport till long after the death of its singer —till it has accrued and incorporated the many passions, many joys and sorrows, it has itself arous'd."[38] Immortality, then, takes time to establish, and art grows into myth, not only because it originates as an embodiment of nature —both biological and cosmic—but because it evolves through its history to embody history itself. According to this evolutionary concept, the poem itself has a history, which parallels but is distinct from the history of its culture. Consequently, just as the "Song of Myself" of 1892 is different from the 1855 version, both versions are different from the "Song of Myself" we now read. Since the man as historical personality disappears in such flux, however, we necessarily come to an understanding of *form* as personality, for the art remains autobiographical. Even as the personality disappears, then, the man as artist endures as form.

Chapter 3
Henry James's Prefaces, or the Story of the Stories

THE SERIES OF PREFACES that Henry James wrote for the New York edition of his works has received scant critical attention, and the handful of critics who have paid any attention to the Prefaces has considered them mainly as literary criticism.[1] Yet to consider the Prefaces solely as criticism is not only to simplify them greatly but to ignore James's suggestion that they "represent, over a considerable course, the continuity of an artist's endeavour, the growth of his whole operative consciousness."[2] Taken together, then, the Prefaces may be seen as the autobiography of an artist—the story or representation of a career. Moreover, as James's revisions of his novels for the New York Edition suggest, the continuity of his career required him to re-see it. Since in James's case the life and the career were closely identified, we witness in the Prefaces the process by which he rewrote his life in writing the story of his career. For writing the life or career necessarily meant rewriting it; in other words, the Prefaces are autobiographical and thus necessarily fictional.

As we have seen, autobiographical writing fictionalizes life by introducing order and establishing connections or relations. In autobiography, then, what was perhaps arbitrary becomes necessary, and in the Prefaces it is precisely the "necessity" of his career that James asserts over and over again. While he intended in the Prefaces partly to develop a critical vocabulary as a means of shaping future criticism of his work, and while he was no doubt motivated by the pleasures of recollection, it was primarily necessity and relatedness that he wished to establish. Indeed, the Prefaces demonstrate the necessity of the form of the individual books, of the project of the New York Edition, of the evolution of James's career as a whole, and, finally and most triumphantly, of the "clumsy Life" surrounding his career. Although we can discuss various parts of James's career separately, his life and art are ultimately one. Since the Prefaces themselves partly establish the wholeness of his career, our divisions must unfortunately be arbitrary, for "thanks to the intimate connexion of things" we have in the Prefaces not only "the story of one's hero" and "the story of one's story itself" (p. 313) but the story of the teller himself.

Whereas criticism reveals art to be artifice, James betrays the special nature of his task in his attempt to prove the "naturalness" of his art. For him, the development of a book is natural and necessary because organic. For example, a book originates with a "seed," a "wind-blown" germ (p. 43), or "a mere grain of subject-matter" (p. 98), which is then "transplanted to richer soil" (p. 122) in the artist's consciousness and, "transferred to the sunny south window-sill of one's fonder attention" (p. 127), subsequently "sprouts," "blooms," and bears fruit according to its nature. Elsewhere the germ-seed imagery becomes less benign. The germ of a story is the vague suggestion "at touch of which the novelist's imagination winces as at the prick of some sharp point: its virtue is all in its needle-like quality." Inoculated with "the virus of suggestion," the disease runs its course in the artist's consciousness (p. 119). Similarly, James describes the creative act in the image of a pearl growing in "the deep well of unconscious cerebration" (p. 23) and in time floating up to the top "with a firm iridescent surface and a notable increase of weight" (p. 23). Fearful of "all disgracefully" betraying "the seam" and showing the "mechanical and superficial" (p. 83), he repeatedly resorts to such organic images in order to prove his novels wholes, in which everything "counts." In the Prefaces, then, James rediscovers the process of creation as organic and thereby imputes something of a historical necessity to the works.

What finally establishes their necessity, however, is James's point of view. His stance in the Prefaces is the position of the author in autobiography. First, he is looking backward and recollecting; second, he is looking inward—that is, his attitude is one of self-consciousness. In looking backward, James does not present the creation of a work as a recollected sequence of events but re-creates it as a process. In the Prefaces to *What Maisie Knew, The*

Wings of the Dove, and *The Ambassadors*, in which he discusses the evolution of the works, he is not even speaking in the past tense at times. Especially in the Preface to *The Ambassadors*, he works backward from the climax and thereby imparts a necessity to the novel's development. Thus, in showing us how a certain book would "logically flower" (p. 143), James presents us with a process of discovery, which may or may not be a faithful reproduction of the book's growth. His mapping out a book's development in terms of an almost logical necessity recalls Poe's "The Philosophy of Composition," for James also characterizes the process as "inductive" (p. 314). As Poe observes, however, "It is only with the *dénouement* constantly in view that we can give a plot its indispensable air of consequence, or causation, by making the incidents . . . tend to the development of the intention."[3] Likewise, James is aware that a retrospective view proves necessity: "Again and yet again, as, from book to book, I proceed with my survey, I find no source of interest equal to this verification after the fact . . . of the scheme of consistency 'gone in' for" (pp. 318–319). By running time backward from the already formed novel, then, James demonstrates the necessity of the choices that he made in order to arrive at that particular novel. In this process, the sequence of events is reversed, the book shrinks back into its seed as in a movie played backward, and, as James writes about *The Ambassadors*, "nothing can exceed the closeness with which the whole fits again into its germ" (p. 308).

Like the retrospective point of view, an attitude of self-consciousness also saves the artist from "the baseness of the *arbitrary* stroke, the touch without its reason" (p. 89). According to Paul Valéry, what makes the novel inferior to poetry and therefore less than art is its arbitrary quality, which results from its unconscious conventions.[4] Consciousness of the artistic conventions that one is using, then, would tend in itself to invest a work with artistic necessity. If, like Poe in "The Philosophy of Composition" and James in the Prefaces, one becomes one's own audience, the accidental and the arbitrary are thereby purged, for whatever is consciously chosen becomes necessary. Thus, while James's imagery imputes a natural growth to his works, his criticism in fact articulates the artifice of the novels.

Self-consciousness, together with James's temporal perspective, generates the controlling principles of his criticism. Consciousness, for example, makes for composition, which is art: "A picture without composition slights its most precious chance for beauty, and is moreover not composed at all unless the painter knows *how* that principle of health and safety, working as an absolutely premeditated art, has prevailed" (p. 84). If consciousness makes for composition, as discrimination and selection it also makes for economy. Life, James writes, "has no direct sense whatever for the subject and is capable, luckily for us, of nothing but splendid waste. Hence the opportunity for the sublime economy of art, which rescues, which saves, and hoards and 'banks,' investing and reinvesting these fruits of toil in wondrous useful 'works' and thus making up for us, desperate spendthrifts that we all naturally are, the most princely of incomes" (p. 120). Economy and "the subtle secrets of that system" preoccupy James in the Prefaces, for the necessity that he discovers in retrospect while proceeding from the book to its creation is, in fact, a perfect economy. Starting with the finished product, he ends up with exactly what he started with, and he can easily meet what he calls "the challenge of economic representation": "To put all that is possible of one's idea into a form and compass that will contain and express it only by delicate adjustments and an exquisite chemistry, so that there will at the end be neither a drop of one's liquor left nor a hair's breadth of the rim of one's glass to spare—every artist will remember how often that sort of necessity has carried with it its particular inspiration" (p. 87). Moreover, "the challenge of economic representation" demanded in turn that consciousness or intelligence become a compositional center, for such a central intelligence would enable James not only to "most economise" the "value" of a character (pp. 37–38) but to "save" the surrounding "lump of life" (p. 120) by casting it in the light of the relations and necessities that consciousness or "appreciation" creates.

James's retrospective point of view in the Prefaces permits him to look at his career as a whole in much the same way that he approaches his novels. To begin with, he is writing from the perspective of mature accomplishment; knowing what he has become, he can interpret the stages of his career as necessary steps in the evolution of the author of *The Ambassadors* and *The Golden Bowl*. James consciously attempts to shape his career around his development of the technique of using the "intelligence" or consciousness of one character as a compositional center. He confesses, "I should even like to give myself the pleasure of retracing from one of my own productions to another the play of a like instinctive disposition, of catching in the fact, at one point after another, from 'Roderick Hudson' to 'The Golden Bowl,' that provision for interest which consists in placing advantageously, placing right in the middle of the light, the most polished of possible mirrors of the subject" (p. 70). Thus Rowland Mallet of *Roderick Hudson* and a character like Christopher Newman of *The American*, who is too typical to be particular, inward, or conscious enough, become the forerunners of a Lambert Strether, who *is* "a mirror verily of miraculous silver" (p. 70).

At times James seems aware of the extent to which his present viewpoint distorts the early books, and he excuses the discrepancy between his statements about the books and the books as they are by claiming that he lacked the art to work out his conceptions. At other times, however, he appears to be quite unaware of how thoroughly he is imposing a present pattern on the past; as a result, his revision of an early work like *The American* reveals a number of lapses in judgment and taste. Yet the patterns that one discovers in looking backward are only half-imposed.

Since a receding temporal perspective serves—like a receding spatial perspective—to subdue details and differences and to reveal instead the larger patterns and agreements, James was to a certain extent truly discovering the shape of his career. Moreover, perhaps even the impositions should be regarded as necessary distortions, for a defined point of view is needed in order to establish connections at all. The nature of the pattern that James discovers in retrospect, then, reflects the present *value* of consciousness for him. Consciousness, which is also James's *method* in the admittedly "monstrous" task of writing the Prefaces (p. 47), thereby becomes the basis not only of his relationship to his heroes but of their relationship to each other.

By a final turn of the screw in the Preface to *The Golden Bowl*, James justifies the Prefaces themselves and the revisions that accompany them. Characteristically recoiling from the arbitrary, James claims in this apology of an apology that his present perspective necessitated the revisions. He insists that he was not working according to some imposed and foreign theory but was simply reading and recording his reading. Thus his "deviations" from the original texts were highly "spontaneous"—"things not of choice, but of immediate and perfect necessity: necessity to the end of dealing with the quantities in question at all" (p. 336). If the past was to be reappropriated at all, and if his works were to mirror *his* consciousness, James had to revise his early books. He in fact admits that the two efforts —rereading and rewriting—"proved to be but one," and he argues that he did not rewrite but merely resaw: ". . . the 'revised' element in the present Edition is . . . these rigid conditions of re-perusal, registered; so many close notes, as who should say, on the particular vision of the matter itself that experience had at last made the only possible one" (p. 339).

In James's view, then, the text was like a mirror—fluid and unformed; if it was to be read at all, it would have to be read as a reflection of the present. This view approximates Wolfgang Iser's conception of the literary work as a virtual meeting place of the author's text and the reader. According to Iser, the work changes between the first and subsequent readings, mainly because the patterns of memory and expectation are different in each reading.[5] In reading his works for the New York Edition, James was reading them with the knowledge, so to speak, of how it all ended. This retrospective view necessitated, then, the re-vision not only of individual books but of the career as a whole, and in both cases James partly discovered and partly imposed the order in each. As Roland Barthes has proposed, a necessary part of the activity of reading is reducing the new and unfamiliar patterns that one encounters in the text to the patterns of more familiar experience that one brought to the reading.[6] In James's case, the relatively unfamiliar earlier work had to be reduced to the more familiar patterns of his later language, style, and form. And James describes the process of revision in similar terms: "It was, all sensibly, as if the clear matter being still there, even as a shining expanse of snow spread over a plain, my exploring tread, for application to it, had quite unlearned the old pace and found itself naturally falling into another, which might sometimes indeed more or less agree with the original tracks, but might most often, or very nearly, break the surface in other places" (p. 336).

The Prefaces represent James's re-vision not simply of his literary career but, more important, of his life. "Our noted behaviour at large," James remarks, "may show for ragged, because it perpetually escapes our control" (p. 348). As autobiography, the Prefaces bring the life itself under artistic control, not in order to justify it but in order precisely to eliminate the need for justification. For he continues, ". . . on all the ground to which the pretension of performance by a series of exquisite laws may apply there reigns one sovereign truth—which decrees that, as art is nothing if not exemplary, care nothing if not active, finish nothing if not consistent, the proved error is the base apologetic deed, the helpless regret is the barren commentary, and 'connexions' are employable for finer purposes than mere gaping contrition" (p. 348). Since James sets out in part to give his life something of the "roundness," wholeness, and necessity of art, the life itself becomes in the Prefaces just such a ground where these "exquisite laws" may apply. He redeems the life partly by seeing it in retrospect as the context for the creation of art and partly by imparting to it—through the self-consciousness of the Prefaces—the quality of art.

Since the attempt to equate life and art informs as much James's personal writing as it does the autobiographical writings of Thoreau and Whitman, we may approach the Prefaces as autobiography by using the terms of the novelist's art. In the Preface to *Roderick Hudson* James writes that experience must organize some system of observation in order to take account of itself. In this project of self-observation or self-consciousness, "everything counts, nothing is superfluous in such a survey; the explorer's note-book strikes me here as endlessly receptive" (p. 3). If experience starts taking notes, so to speak, it acquires a center around which to gather itself. For James, the art of representation was a way in which experience shaped itself, saved itself, and made itself count simply by being conscious of itself. More important, art saved as well the individual life that went into its creation—"the accidents and incidents of its growth" (p. 7). He writes: "This accordingly is what I mean by the contributive value—or put it simply as, to one's own sense, the beguiling charm—of the *accessory* facts in a given artistic case. This is why, as one looks back, the private history of any sincere work, however modest its pretensions, looms with its own completeness in the rich, ambiguous aesthetic air, and seems at once to borrow a dignity and to mark, so to say, a station" (pp. 3–4).

The Prefaces themselves should also be seen as experience taking note of itself, for in their self-consciousness as a "re-presentation" of the creative process, they make "everything count" and thereby rescue the "clumsy Life" that surrounds the art. Since necessity is the saving principle of art, all the events that can be brought into a relation with the creation of art are saved from contingency and become necessary rather than arbitrary. Thus, whereas seen as recollection the Prefaces demonstrate the necessity of James's individual works and his entire career, seen as self-consciousness they argue for the necessity of the "accessory facts" or the history. From the retrospective and self-conscious viewpoint of autobiography, then, life partakes of the quality of art, for the necessity that life achieves in retrospect and in the light of consciousness is, in fact, the economy that is the very life, according to James, of the art of representation. Life comes to count, therefore, when it achieves economy—that is, when it becomes a unified, self-sufficient whole. At this point, however, it becomes art, since the principle of economy is—as we have seen—basic to James's conception of his art: "There is life and life, and as waste is only life sacrificed and thereby prevented from 'counting,' I delight in a deep-breathing economy and an organic form" (p. 84).

Moreover, in the Prefaces the art not only makes the life relevant but can be said, in fact, to make the life. James looks back from the work and creates the life that must have been there in order for him to create the work in the first place. In the Preface to *The Tragic Muse*, for example, he discusses the origins of his conception: "What I make out from furthest back is that I must have had from still further back, must in fact practically have always had, the happy thought of some dramatic picture of the 'artist-life.' . . . To 'do something about art' . . . must have been for me early a good deal of a nursed intention" (p. 79). Just as the fact of a particular novel necessitates the "accidents" of its growth, the existence of the novels taken together shapes the life as a whole, for they *are* the connections and relations that give it continuity. "We are condemned," James writes, "whether we will or no, to abandon and outlive, to forget and disown and hand over to desolation, many vital or social performances—if only because the traces, records, connexions, the very memorials we would fain preserve, are practically impossible to rescue for that purpose from the general mixture." Whereas acts become disconnected from their actor, works of art remain connected, for "our relation to them is essentially traceable, and in that fact abides, we feel, the incomparable luxury of the artist." The "luxury" of the artist, then, is freedom from the past: "It rests altogether with himself not to break with his values, not to 'give away' his importances. Not to *be* disconnected, for the tradition of behaviour, he has but to feel that he is not; by his lightest touch the whole chain of relation and responsibility is reconstituted. . . . All of which means for him conduct with a vengeance, since it is conduct minutely and publicly attested" (p. 348). Since the Prefaces recollect and reconstitute the "whole chain of relation and responsibility" between the artist and his works, and since the works make "relevant" the accidents of their growth, the Prefaces "minutely and publicly" redeem not only the art but the life from time and accident.

While in their self-observation and recollection the Prefaces more or less consciously discover connections, by virtue of their form they necessarily fictionalize the past, for James casts them not as criticism but as first-person narrative or, to use his words, as a "story of one's story." In the Preface to *Roderick Hudson*, he admits that "really, universally, relations stop nowhere, and the exquisite problem of the artist is eternally but to draw, by a geometry of his own, the circle within which they shall happily *appear* to do so" (p. 5). The "continuity of things," then, is never broken save in art or re-presentation. Since narration itself establishes connections and the limits—arbitrary and artificial—of relatedness, the order, cohesion, or wholeness that the Prefaces give to James's career and that any autobiography gives to the career of its writer is, in the end, a literary creation. Moreover, the continuously present consciousness or personality that autobiography creates is likewise a function of narrative, for just as one must set down or narrate an event for it to assume shape and order, one must also *tell* one's story in order for it to be one's own. Insofar as life is a different entity from what Whitman calls the "mere fact consciousness," it is a creation of words or a story we tell ourselves. Since the telling imposes too rigid orders of causality and development on the life, however, it distorts the life, yet without this distortion there would be no past, for it is the telling that discovers a life as *related* and as *ours*. Thus if a narrative structure is necessarily fictional, it is also basic to the conception of life in a given language, and for this reason we conceive of our lives in the image of fiction.

Representation or the telling of events necessarily fictionalizes life, because narratives have beginnings and endings. As Roquentin in Sartre's *Nausea* laments, "Nothing happens while you live. The scenery changes, people come in and go out, that's all. There are no beginnings."[7] It is in narrative that things "happen," for narration establishes beginnings and endings and draws the arbitrary "circle" around events. When beginnings and endings are fixed, however, the flow of time is reversed. Events happen in one direction, Roquentin continues, but we relate them in the opposite direction: "The story is going on backwards: moments have stopped piling themselves happy-go-luckily one on top of the other, they are caught up by the end of the story which draws them on and each one of them in turn the previous moment."[8] The telling of any event, then, not only saves it from the unremitting, forward flow of time but sends it running back upstream. Consequently, insofar as our conscious life is a process of talking to ourselves continuously, we are living double lives, and our conscious existence is, in its temporal structure, a fictional existence. In the story that we tell ourselves, time runs backward, even as biological and historical time goes forward.

Since from a retrospective viewpoint time runs backward, the course of events becomes necessary in the telling. Moreover, since all narration has a retrospective viewpoint, art itself becomes necessary only in the story that one tells of it, and without the story of the story the art is an arbitrary construct. Paul Valéry, who in his practice of self-observation resembles James, writes, "Perhaps it would be interesting, *just once*, to write a work which at each juncture would show the diversity of solutions that can present themselves to the mind and from which it *chooses* the unique sequel to be found in the text. To do this would be to substitute for the illusion of a unique scheme which imitates reality that of the *possible-at-each-moment*, which I think more truthful."[9] Thus Valéry acknowledges the essentially arbitrary nature of any poem; in his view, a poem represents only a momentary order, which is always in danger of disintegrating in the confusion of daily language. James likewise is aware of the arbitrary nature of art, for to state that, ideally, relations stop nowhere amounts to saying that they may stop anywhere one wishes. Since the Prefaces argue for the necessity of the art, however, we may conclude that events—life, art—become necessary only in retrospect and in narration, for it is only in narration that we have significant connections and relations. The double meaning of "relation," then, is telling, for the relation or narration of a life is not a search for relations between possibly disparate events but is itself the relation or relatedness of the events. Narrative makes for connectedness not only because it is retrospective but because it reflects—if it is to remain readable—connections universal to a culture. According to Barthes, the most convincing narrative sequence is "the most 'cultural' sequence where one immediately recognizes a host of previous reading and conversation patterns."[10] Thus the connections that narration establishes are necessarily public and, therefore, justified, for a personal or private narrative logic is as impossible as a private language.

Barthes suggests further that this "readability" of the classical narrative lies in its "irreversibility."[11] Indeed, "to relate" derives from *referre* or "to bring back," and in the narrating of a recollection we arrive at irreversibility, for the present or even the future of what is being narrated has already become a past for the narrator. And it is this

irreversibility that constitutes the fatedness of autobiographical narrative: an end point that is already reached
gives shape to the past. Precisely because the present end
point shapes the past, however, the past remains free or
reinterpretable and reusable, for it changes with each successive present. This conception of the past as free within
its fatedness approximates James's vision of the past as a
place, in Georges Poulet's words, "where one can not only
recapture oneself but where one can also recapture 'the
possible development of one's own nature one mayn't have
missed.' "[12] It is in these terms that Poulet reads Strether's
adventure; transported from one continent to another,
Strether "at the same time transports with him the possibility of another Strether 'buried for years in dark corners'
which is going to 'sprout again under forty-eight hours of
Paris.' "[13] Strether, then, is not living his present—the future of the choices that he made in the past—but a past
possibility or the future of a choice that he in fact did not
make in the past. In refusing to tell Chad what to do, Strether is no longer the man he is but the man he might have
been, and James's going back in time to revise books that
were written some thirty years earlier shows his past to be
as fluid as Strether's.

Finally, it is due to the nature of memory itself that the
past is fictionalized in the Prefaces in particular and in
autobiography in general. According to Edmund Husserl,
recollection is also shaped by the present, because memory
is "oriented" toward "the future of the recollected." Every
act of memory, Husserl writes, "contains intentions of expectation whose fulfillment leads to the present." Thus, "as
the recollective process advances, [its] . . . horizon is continually opened up anew and becomes richer and more
vivid. In view of this, the horizon is filled with recollected
events which are always new. Events which formerly were
only foreshadowed are now quasi-present, seemingly in
the mode of the embodied present."[14] Memory, then, cannot recapture primary perception, for as the future of the
perception comes to open up, the past correspondingly ex-

pands. Consequently, distortions like consciously or unconsciously selective memory, polemical pleading, or, in Daniel Aaron's phrase, "ancestor worship" of the "living relic" who is his or her own ancestor[15] are simply conscious or unconscious exaggerations of the basic distortion of narrative. Distortions of the so-called content, therefore, merely reflect the formal patterns of retrospective narration.

Since autobiography is not only a retrospective but a self-conscious and self-referring mode, it is riddled as well with the distortions that style engenders. In autobiography in general and in James in particular, the distant past—when checked against the biographer's data—is always more distorted than the recent past, both because present choices of patterns and significances tend to color the past and because the style of the writing more closely resembles the personality of the recent past. James's mature style in the Prefaces changes his earlier work, and since style determines the form of experience, there are technical as well as psychological reasons for selective memory. As a result, the changes that James's later style effects are necessary if not—when recorded in his revisions—always altogether happy, for it is the present style that in fact makes the past his. James admits that in retrospect the works hardly seem to be his, because their " 'private' character . . . quite insists on dropping out" (p. 4). He can revive his relation to his early works, however, by reappropriating them in his new style. Thus revision becomes, in his words, an "act of re-appropriation" (p. 336), and what he is doing in the Prefaces may be called criticism only if we use his definition: "To criticise is to appreciate, to appropriate, to take intellectual possession, to establish in fine a relation with the criticised thing and make it one's own" (p. 155). Moreover, the past becomes conceivable and real—that is, a part of the way in which one in fact perceives and experiences the world—through the imposition of the present style. By re-collecting events in one present style and form, autobiography makes of the life one life. Once again, then, an autobiography is not a search for order but is itself the order

of the life, because it is in written language. It is an order
that relates the facts, because it is a narrative; accordingly,
it is an order that makes the life one's own life, because it
has the unity of style. Finally, it is an order that humanizes,
for by speaking in the public and inherited language of literature, the individual in autobiography places her or his
history in its social and cultural context.

In the Preface to *Roderick Hudson*, James writes of himself as the artist: "Addicted to 'stories' and inclined to retrospect, he fondly takes, under this backward view, his
whole unfolding, his process of production, for a thrilling
tale, almost for a wondrous adventure, only asking himself
at what stage of remembrance the mark of the relevant
will begin to fail. He frankly proposes to take this mark
everywhere for granted" (p. 4). This passage introduces
the recurrent imagery of adventure that James uses to describe his career. *He* is the hero of the tale that he is now
telling, and he is able to "show" *his* "several actions beau-
tifully become one" (p. 88), for everything that he remembers is not only relevant but of a piece. We can describe
James's adventure in the Prefaces in the same terms that
he applies to his creation of fictional characters, because
the Prefaces record more than one adventure. In recounting the story of *The Ambassadors*, for example, James
charts not only the unfolding of Strether's adventure but
the progress of his own adventure—"the thrilling ups and
downs, the intricate ins and outs of the compositional
problem" (p. 319). More important, the Preface itself
represents the adventure of now telling how he came to
tell Strether's story; as James writes, ". . . it comes to me
again and again, over this licentious record, that one's bag
of adventures . . . has been only half-emptied by the mere
telling of one's story" (p. 313). The story of the story remained to be told, not only for "the joy of living over, as a
chapter of experience, the particular intellectual adventure" (p. 29) but for the "confirmed infatuation of retrospect," which made even of the "usual difficulties" a record

for James to "fairly cherish as some adventurer in another line may hug the sense of his inveterate habit of just saving in time the neck he ever undiscourageably risks" (p. 85). In this adventure of recollection, each book is a chapter, the career the "thrilling tale," and James its self-made hero.[16]

In the Preface to *The Tragic Muse*, however, James explains that an artist cannot properly be a fictional hero. The artist's "triumph," he claims, "is but the triumph of what he produces," and "his romance is the romance he himself projects." Consequently, the "privilege of the hero— that is of the martyr or of the interesting and appealing and comparatively floundering *person*—places him in quite a different category, belongs to him only as to the artist deluded, diverted, frustrated or vanquished" (pp. 96–97). However, since in personal or autobiographical writing one tells the story of one's own romance, one can become a hero, for now we see an artist not with back turned to us "as he bends over his work" (p. 96) but facing us in a repetition of an artist's original relation to the text. We see the hero in action, as it were, because novels, James asserts, are acts of the highest order: ". . . to 'put' things is very exactly and responsibly and interminably to do them. Our expression of them, and the terms on which we understand that, belong as nearly to our conduct and our life as every other feature of our freedom" (p. 347). Although these acts may be diverse, disparate, and unconnected in time and place, there is always the presence of the hero to pull them together. James's consciousness, then, is not only the form but the organizing principle of the Prefaces, and everything that it comprehends thereby becomes significant and relevant. Thus consciousness itself is relation: as Saint Augustine remarks about *his* task of recollection, to find relations or "to collect" is the meaning of "to think" (*cogitare*).[17]

James, therefore, is a hero on the model of his characters. Self-consciousness redeems the lives of his characters from the vulgarity of the arbitrary and accidental, because self-consciousness amounts to choosing one's fate. His heroes meet him halfway, for they were patterned after the artist in the first place. For example, Hyacinth Robinson's experience of London in *The Princess Casamassima* reflects James's own experience of the city, and James portrays him "watching very much as I had watched" (p. 60). James's characters, then, mirror their author: it is their awareness that "*makes* absolutely the intensity of their adventure" (p. 62), because their adventures—like James's—are inward. Yet his heroes are self-conscious in a more conventional sense. Writing about a type in American literature, Mary McCarthy observes that such characters leave the United States and go to Europe in order to impersonate figures in a novel.[18] She includes in this group Isabel Archer, but her observation would apply to many of James's characters, whose lives thus become doubly fictional. Moreover, for James's protagonists as well as for James, consciousness makes life count, because it makes for economy. His calling his intelligent "centres" "registers" and "reflectors" recalls the theme of economy. A character like Milly Theale is as expert in economy as any artist: life *is* wealth, and she must economize on it. James's characters in general know the value of economy and deplore waste, and each is something of an artist or a person "on whom nothing is lost."[19] Thus compression and composition, which save art from becoming "vulgar," also save life by making life as well as art necessary.

Perhaps self-consciousness, which is the mode of the Prefaces, necessarily involves the projection of the self as hero. Self-consciousness is awareness of oneself as a particular person and, at the same time, as part of—even representative of—a species. Likewise, literary self-consciousness, which creates the sense of personality, also projects the personality as a representative hero in the same act. For example, if one says, "I think, therefore I am," or, in more Jamesian terms, "I am aware, therefore I am alive," one becomes conscious of oneself not only as doing the particular act of thinking or being aware but as belonging to a species which *is* by thinking or being aware. In this way self-consciousness becomes representative and hero-ic. As consciousness, therefore, James is universal; his particularity lies only in his "relations" with his works. No less than Thoreau and Whitman, then, James "dared"—as Emerson observes about Dante—"to write his autobiography in colossal cipher, or into universality."[20]

Self-consciousness not only makes the self a hero and its experience a related whole but involves the same reversal of time that characterizes life as re-presented in literature. For the self-conscious self-observer, each event happens twice, for if one is self-conscious, what one says or does has already happened once in the consciousness. Thus the actual happening of the event is a re-presentation or repetition, and life comes to assume the quality of art. As Kierkegaard has written, one's "own consciousness raised to the second power is repetition."[21] And repetition, in turn, makes for art, for "the affair of the painter is not the immediate, it is the reflected field of life, the realm not of application, but of *appreciation*" (p. 65). Since representation or repetition makes for relations and thus constitutes the subject of the painter of life—"the related state, to each other, of certain figures and things" (p. 5)—we may well say of the poet or artist that, in Wallace Stevens's words, "The man-hero is not the exceptional monster, / But he that of repetition is most master."[22] If repetition makes for relatedness or art, James's Prefaces, which represent his career, make the career itself a work of art. Consequently, the impulse for "inward mastery of the outward experience" that, in R. P. Blackmur's phrase, characterizes James's heroes[23] also informs not only the Prefaces but all autobiographical writing, for it is through self-consciousness, repetition, and representation that "clumsy Life" is mastered. In other words, self-consciousness or awareness of life as lived is a representation of the temporal process of living, and auto-biography represents this repetition. Self-consciousness, then, provides the continuity of life as a temporal process, much as primary memory provides the temporal continuity in reading a book. In the writing of autobiography, this immediate or primary self-consciousness is superseded by a secondary self-consciousness, which recollects the perceptions of primary self-consciousness. Again, this relationship resembles the difference between remembering chapter 1 of a book while reading chapter 2 and recollecting the entire book after finishing it.

In the Prefaces James resembles a god looking into a mirror and finding himself reflected in his creations, the genesis of which he is in the process of recounting. As he describes Strether and subsequently characterizes himself (pp. 320, 335), he is both hero and historian, conscious and retrospective. The image of a mirror, which James continually uses to describe the consciousness of his characters, reflects his position as well. In fact, he would make of himself a mirror in order to reflect and represent all he sees. In his insatiable desire to "do" everything that he sees, the "common air" comes to him for him to "taste" of " 'subjects' and situations, character and history, the tragedy and comedy of life" (p. 59), and as he stalks the "tragedy and comedy of life," "possible stories, presentable figures, rise from the thick jungle . . . fluttering up like startled game" (p. 60). Thus James is as inclusive as Whitman and shares, in Quentin Anderson's words, Whitman's "imperial self,"[24] because for James, too, the world is full of "dumb, beautiful ministers" awaiting their voices. The image of a mirror, then, appropriately conveys James's idea of the artist's task as not original creation but reflection, representation, or repetition. Just as in *What Maisie Knew* Maisie's consciousness transforms "appearances in themselves vulgar and empty enough" (p. 147) into a semblance of dignity by connecting them with universals, the artist's consciousness reflects the surrounding life, which thereby becomes interesting and acquires value. Passive and receptive, then, the mind is for James "a reflecting and colouring medium" (p. 67).

Since the mind as mirror gains content only in reflecting, the patterns of its discovery are inseparable from the patterns that it discovers. For example, James writes of Maggie in *The Golden Bowl*, ". . . the Princess . . . in addition to feeling everything she has to, and to playing her part just in that proportion, duplicates, as it were, her value and becomes a compositional resource, and of the finest order, as well as a value intrinsic" (p. 329). As consciousness, then, she provides James with his subject *and* his form. Likewise, in the Prefaces his own consciousness not only provides him—retrospectively—with his subject but constitutes the form of his autobiographical writing. In his "irrepressible and insatiable, his extravagant and immoral" interest in "the 'nature' of a mind" (p. 156), the mind became for James both his subject and his form, with the result that words became his acts as well as the tools of his art.

Consequently, as readers or critics we face two difficulties. First, the autobiographer's tools of observation—language, structure, and style—affect the past life or the facts observed. Second, in James's case the facts and the instruments of observation are phenomena of the same order, for the life that is recalled is one not of acts but of words. Thus it becomes meaningless to question the truth of James's account, because testing the truth of his observations would be like testing the accuracy of a yardstick with another yardstick. On top of all this, our method of discussing the Prefaces is equally controlled by the language and verbal structures. Even more, our very experience of James's Prefaces shares the point of view that informed his experience, for as readers or critics we also are retrospective and relate what we have read in a limited number of distinct patterns, which we partly impose and partly discover. Finally, whereas reading is a function of primary consciousness, writing about a work is an act of self-consciousness, which, one hopes, is also an act of awareness.

Chapter 4
Henry Adams,
Connoisseur of Chaos

"In plain words," Henry Adams concludes toward the end of his search for unity, "Chaos was the law of nature; Order was the dream of man,"[1] and his readers have generally agreed with this assessment of the way things are. Yet it would make just as much sense to maintain, for example, that chaos is the projection of the human mind onto nature and that order is the law of nature. Indeed, our perspective becomes inclusive enough to comprehend *The Education of Henry Adams* only when we balance Adams's statements with their antitheses. Although this approach may involve us in ambiguities and contradictions, it would have Adams's approval, for in his view education or "interesting" education has a good deal to do with confusion. In fact, Adams would have reformed the educational system by undermining its happy one-mindedness: "He would have seated a rival assistant professor opposite him, whose business should be strictly limited to expressing opposite views" (pp. 303–304). The project proved impossible, however, since "no irregularity shocked the intellectual atmosphere so much as contradiction or competition between teachers" (p. 304). Yet Adams's kind of education would be at least as useful as the traditional kind. For example, such an education would be scientific, since "science gets on only by adopting different theories, sometimes contradictory" (p. 497). If two contradictory theories explain a given phenomenon, the scientist makes use of both. In a sense, then, Adams's own education consists of learning to live with the contradictions that make experience whole. Thus "conflict, competition, contradiction" (p. 303), which, according to Adams, *his* mind required, do not engender multiplicity but make precisely for unity.

Adams's idea of the uses of contradiction approaches Kenneth Burke's concept of "perspective by incongruity" or "planned incongruity," which can be helpful in understanding the *Education*. Burke, who derives his theory from Henri Bergson, argues that experience is continuous and whole. Accordingly, metaphysicians "solve" only pseudo-problems, for their syntheses join logical or conceptual dis-

tinctions, which neither derive from nor are justified by
the nature of the universe. In other words, they synthesize
the purely verbal distinctions that we have created in our
attempts to talk about reality. Burke joins Bergson in pro-
posing that we "deliberately cultivate the use of contradictory concepts" as "the nearest *verbal* approach to reality."
Burke asserts, for example, that we "should not—as phi-
losophers—speak of an anabolistic process in an organism
as wholly distinct from a katabolistic one, thereat plaguing
ourselves to find a schema for joining them and getting
metabolism." If a synthetic term does not already exist, it
can always be invented by combining antithetical words,
as in the terms "space-time" and "mind-body." Thus, instead of searching for a Hegelian synthesis to follow thesis
and antithesis, the philosopher should realize that "the real
course of events is necessarily, at all times, unified"—that
it *is* the synthesis.[2]

I propose, then, to consider the *Education* from a perspective by incongruity, for this method enjoys the ad-
vantage of being Adams's own method. "From earliest
childhood," he writes, "the boy was accustomed to feel that,
for him, life was double" (p. 9). Having "inherited his
double nature" (p. 9), the child saw it reflected in the
world around him, and "the double exterior nature gave
life its relative values. Winter and summer, cold and heat,
town and country, force and freedom, marked two modes
of life and thought, balanced like lobes of the brain" (p.
7). Adams insists that the violent contrasts of "exterior
nature" were real, and "the man who pretended they were
not, was in his eyes a schoolmaster—that is, a man employed to tell lies to little boys" (p. 9). Yet he compares
these "real," external oppositions to the "lobes of the brain,"
and this reference to the brain's double structure suggests
that the perceiving mind may have contributed to Adams's
organizing experience in dualities rather than in cycles,
say, or in some other pattern. From the schoolboy's division of seasons to the older man's opposition of the Virgin
and the Dynamo, it is Adams's *thought* that proceeds in

pairs, doubles, and mirrorings. For this reason, the final syntheses—whether of life, education, or force—that the *Education* embodies have the wholeness—the multiplicity —of the syntheses that *are*.

We can see the *Education* as unitary and as a whole only by approaching it from many directions at once. Adams's multiplicity deserves more than lip service, not only because words are "slippery" and thought is "viscous" but because he consciously and consistently serves a number of different masters at the same time. A major failing of Adams's readers has been their inability to accept his multiplicity. The *Education* has been read as class rhetoric and as a literary portrait of the Romantic antihero; as a chronicle of the disintegration of liberalism and as the diary of the "disintegration of a mind"; and as autobiography and as anything but autobiography.[3] The extremes to which Adams drives some of his undertakers indicate that it is necessary to formulate a *method* of reading the *Education*. Discussing the *Education* in terms of various and contradictory models and vocabularies may enable us to avoid some of the excesses of Adams criticism. Our models—whether historical, autobiographical, or literary— will necessarily introduce different perspectives, and the knowledge that we are *introducing* division should help us to keep in mind that as an event the *Education* is a unity.

To be consistent with our own method, however, we must recognize that the *Education* is, in fact, a deeply divided book. Adams's method of working through opposites reflects, after all, divided loyalties. Once again, Kenneth Burke comes to the rescue and quotes C. K. Ogden: "Clearness and consecutiveness of thinking . . . depends primarily upon clearness in our interests." Ogden traces blunders of thought, as well as the "extraordinary views of many demented persons," to confused, mixed, or eccentric interests.[4] Confused or mixed interests, then, may account for Adams's practice of continually undercutting himself. As we shall see, the suicidal nature of this method is very congenial to him and is part of a larger pattern in the *Edu-*

cation. Yet the *Education* is so compelling and so much more than "confused" partly because Adams is aware of the confusion in his interests and succeeds, if not in resolving his dilemmas, at least in learning to live with them by progressively enlarging his perspective. Accordingly, it is fitting that we should tailor our method to Adams and proceed by undercutting ourselves, yet we may allow ourselves, finally, a positive synthesis, especially since *we* are not suicidal.

For a modest man, Adams is not shy about drawing parallels between himself and mythic, literary, or historical personages. By punning, he identifies himself with Adam and becomes archetypal man; as hero of the *Education*, he has various prototypes, from the wanderers Odysseus and Rasselas to Teufelsdröckh, Faust, and Hamlet; and as author he compares himself to Saint Augustine, Dante, Shakespeare, and Gibbon. It would be interesting to follow up any one of these associations. For example, Dante also saw his life as broken in half and, like Adams, wrote a cosmology out of personal motives, partly in order to settle personal accounts. It is the figure of Hamlet, however, that is the most useful in illuminating the many aspects of Adams's hero.[5] To begin with, Hamlet is the heir apparent dispossessed of his kingship, and Adams casts himself in the same role. In a way, what we have in the first chapter of the *Education* is a number of ghosts claiming Adams's loyalty and even giving an air of legitimacy to the child's expectation that he, too, would be president one day. Moreover, the child was not simply naïve, as Adams would have us believe, for the theme of dispossession or disinheritance in the later chapters serves to validate the child's claim: he, "American of Americans, with Heaven knew how many Puritans and Patriots behind him," was "no worse off than the Indians or the buffalo who had been ejected from their heritage by his own people" (p. 238). Adams's blaming President Grant personally for putting an end to his political ambitions continues this theme by casting Grant as the usurper.

Like Hamlet, however, Adams is both in and out of the game. While he has responsibilities to his name, his past, and his class, he is at the same time curiously detached from such obligations, for the second half of the nineteenth century is no time for an Adams. His complaint that he was born in the wrong century recalls Hamlet's lament:

> The time is out of joint: O cursed spite,
> That ever I was born to set it right!

Adams's hero is aware that action is demanded, but he cannot act with rationality and purpose any more than can Hamlet. In Adams's poem "Buddha and Brahma," the rajah's son asks his father:

> . . . Life for me is thought,
> But, were it action, how, in youth or age,
> Can man act wisely, leaving thought aside?

The father's advice is, "*Think not! Strike!*"[6] Similarly, whether he is slaying Polonius or going for Laertes's throat, Hamlet's action is always a thoughtless violence, for he is paralyzed when he thinks. Adams faces the same alternatives, since "to one who is still in the world even if not of it, doubts are as plenty as days" (p. 161). Baffled whether one should be Guelph or Ghibelline, he advises, "Better take sides first, and reason about it for the rest of life" (p. 84). Yet he could not take his own advice, for as he wrote to Charles Francis Adams, "The more I see, the more I am convinced that a man whose mind is balanced like mine, in such a way that what is evil never seems unmixed with good, and what is good always streaked with evil; an object seems never important enough to call out strong energies till they are exhausted, nor necessary enough not to allow of its failure being possible to retrieve; in short, a mind which is not strongly positive and absolute, cannot

be steadily successful in action."[7] Thus Adams continually
fluctuated between involvement and detachment, because
his alternatives were blind action and silence. Of course,
what plagues both Adams and Hamlet is self-consciousness
and the double perspective that it creates:

> Thus conscience does make cowards of us all;
> And thus the native hue of resolution
> Is sicklied o'er with the pale cast of thought,
> And enterprises of great pitch and moment
> With this regard their currents turn awry,
> And lose the name of action.

Adams knows that Hamlet's withering self-consciousness
is at bottom suicidal, for he is aware of Narcissus's fate:
"Nearly all the highest intelligence known to history had
drowned itself in the reflection of its own thought" (p.
432). Adams tries to put up some resistance: *he* "had no
need to learn from Hamlet the fatal effect of the pale cast
of thought on enterprises great or small. He had no notion
of letting the currents of his action be turned awry by this
form of conscience. To him, the current of his time was to
be his current, lead where it might" (p. 232). This is his
answer in 1867; in the end, however, he is closer to Hamlet than not, for the *Education* is, after all, the story of his
self-consciousness and passivity: "As it happened, he never
got to the point of playing the game at all; he lost himself
in the study of it, watching the errors of the players; but
this is the only interest in the story, which otherwise has no
moral and little incident" (p. 4). Adams admits that as a
young man he was "a nervous animal, [who] made life a
terror by seeing too much" (p. 167), and to the end his
terrors as well as his pleasures remain those of a spectator:
"He felt quite well satisfied to look on, and from time to
time he thought he might risk a criticism of the players"
(p. 323).

No less than Hamlet, however, Adams ultimately acts,
for the *Education*, as he later claimed, was itself an education for him.[8] He wrote his own "play," in which he cast

not only himself but his audience or his future readers, for
he also wrote in order to "hold, as 't were, the mirror up
to nature" and to show "the very age and body of the time
his form and pressure." If he was unable to shape his age
for the present, he could shape it for the future. Perhaps
the future was what really interested Adams all along, for
his education, if successful, would have enabled him to live
literally one step ahead of time. Education, as he conceived
it, had less to do with life as lived than with finding a system that would account for the future. By discovering a
principle that would make the passage of time a meaningful *sequence*, one could predict what to expect, and knowing what to expect, one could "react with vigor and economy." It is this economizing of one's energies that would
constitute, in Adams's terms, education (pp. 314–315). In
a discontinuous universe, however, this kind of education
becomes impossible, and Adams's attempts to live one step
ahead of time—"to keep in front of the movement, and, if
necessary, lead it to chaos" (p. 403)—did in fact lead him
to chaos.

Adams's complaint that his education did not prepare
him for the twentieth century does not seem quite justified;
chronologically speaking, he no more belonged to the twentieth century than we belong to the twenty-first. Since it
was the future that he meant to control, however, he succeeded in making himself into a twentieth-century figure.
His own work, then, is another manifestation of "the motive influence, old or new, which raised both Pyramids and
Cross"—the "attraction of power in a future life" (p. 482).
Just as Adams's theory of history maps out the future, the
Education as a whole is addressed to historians of the
future, and it is in these terms that the concluding sentences of the book, for example, may be read. And the
Education has in fact succeeded in influencing historiography; it has become the history of its age. In our attempt
to study the late nineteenth century, we are trapped, in
Edward Lurie's words, in the "web of deception" that its
contemporaries—notably Henry Adams—wove in describ-

ing it. According to Lurie, historians of the period too readily accept the comfortable symbol of the Gilded Age, for "if Adams believed, short-sightedly, that America had become a multiplicity of forces impervious to individual control or determination, he had done much from his new power base in Washington to create that energy-machine he seemed, on the surface, to despise." Adams, then, may be seen in the *Education* as speaking for a network of elitist alliances that controlled politics, diplomacy, and culture in the late nineteenth century.[9]

This view of the *Education* is somewhat limited, however, for if Adams had more power in the game than he would have us believe, he also had less power than he would have liked. His education consists largely of learning to come to terms with authority and force, and the *Education* represents his symbolic mastery—through repetition—of a series of necessary defeats. For example, he centers the re-creation of his childhood around his relation to authority. Even the child's relation to nature becomes a reflection of his relation to power; whereas summer is license, winter means school, constraint, and obedience. From schoolmasters to his grandfather, the whole universe "combined to crush a child," for "a boy's will is his life, and he dies when it is broken, as the colt dies in harness, taking a new nature in becoming tame. Rarely has the boy felt kindly towards his tamers" (p. 12). The "pilgrim of power," who seeks to divine the ways of force whether natural, political, mechanical, or supernatural, sets out in a sense to redeem the child, who had to accept "necessary defeat." Adams's quest, then, is partly psychological, for his assessment of himself is at stake.

It is for this reason that his feelings about personal power remain curiously mixed. In a telling phrase, Adams writes that John Hay, dying at the height of power, would not fade into "cheap obscurity" (p. 504). Power, fame, and money form a cluster, and to the end Adams is ambivalent toward all of them. His statement that "sixty years afterwards he was still unable to make up his mind" (p. 22) between State Street and Quincy is closer to the truth than not. Moreover, while he refuses actively to pursue money or political power, he seems to resent that *he* is not "rolling in millions" and that no one offers *him* any office. Perhaps his ambivalence toward political power is partly a result of his feeling inadequate to the expectations for himself that he has inherited. In a sense, he remains as dwarfed and as "paralyzed by awe" as he was when his grandfather took him by the hand and walked him to school (p. 13). Adams begins the *Education* by playing up his smallness, for in the midst of looming family associations is little Henry: ". . . the First Church, the Boston State House, Beacon Hill, John Hancock and John Adams, Mount Vernon Street and Quincy, all crowding on ten pounds of unconscious baby-hood" (pp. 3–4). As if all this were not enough to have to measure up to, he was handicapped by illness and "fell behind his brothers two or three inches in height, and proportionally in bone and weight" (p. 6). Indeed, Adams repeatedly associates power and strength of will with size. As "manikin" or "little man," he is powerless in the face of overwhelming forces; in a character like Senator Ratcliffe in *Democracy*, however, physical and political power coincide, for the "Prairie Giant of Peonia"—the most powerful man in the Senate—was "a great, ponderous man, over six feet high." On the other hand, the reformer French—of whom Ratcliffe gets the better—is portrayed as ridiculous partly because of his size: French "lost no occasion of impressing his views; but unluckily he was a very light weight, and his manner was a little ridiculous."[10] Similarly, Adams can take his own size lightly: ". . . in the mission attached to Mr. Adams in 1861, the only rag of legitimacy or order was the private secretary, whose stature was not sufficient to impose awe on the Court and Parliament of Great Britain" (p. 113).

I have tried to suggest only that Adams might have felt somewhat inadequate to his expectations of and for himself as an Adams, yet the same evidence may be seen also as his strategy for escaping his place in history. Once again, Hamlet provides an appropriate model, for while he knows political power to be only mortal, he also knows that to reject it reveals a certain inadequacy. For example, an exchange on the nature of worldly ambition follows Hamlet's calling Denmark a prison:

> *Rosencrantz:* Why then, your ambition makes it one; 'tis too narrow for your mind.
>
> *Hamlet:* O God, I could be bounded in a nutshell and count myself a king of infinite space, were it not that I have bad dreams.
>
> *Guildenstern:* Which dreams indeed are ambition, for the very substance of the ambitious is merely the shadow of a dream.
>
> *Hamlet:* A dream itself is but a shadow.
>
> *Rosencrantz:* Truly, and I hold ambition of so airy and light a quality that it is but a shadow's shadow.
>
> *Hamlet:* Then are our beggars bodies, and our monarchs and outstretched heroes the beggars' shadows. Shall we to the court? for, by my fay, I cannot reason.

Hamlet's reason breaks down here, because the logical conclusion of Guildenstern's argument is unacceptable to him, and some lines later he remarks, "Beggar that I am . . . ." Thus, while Hamlet would be a "king of infinite space," he is troubled by "bad dreams," for it is beggarly of a prince not to have ambition and power. From the heights of his protective irony, Adams also reveals that he has misgivings. He writes that he never held office because "no President had ever invited him to fill one. The reason was good, and was also conveniently true, but left open an awkward doubt of his morals or capacity" (p. 322). For as William Jordy concludes, "It was not lack of office . . . which measured failure so much as his paralysis at the idea."[11] Indeed, "paralysis" is a word that is crucial to understanding Adams; it not only relates him to Hamlet but recalls Kierkegaard's definition of irony as the expression of being paralyzed by anxiety.[12] Such, then, is the context of Adams's attitude toward himself, for the irony of statements like "he was for sale, in the open market," he was "cheap," and he was "to be bought at the price of a mechanic" (p. 240) must cut both ways.

In order to complement our use of a literary model with an awareness of Adams's historical situation, however, we should also assume that he was, in fact, the strict moralist of the *Education* and that he recoiled from the corruption which power brings in its wake. He resembles his hero in *Democracy*, Madeleine Lee, who talks like a realist but, in the final analysis, is too fastidious to be one. As a "pilgrim of power," Adams chooses to stand in the wings and, by studying power and by ridiculing those who seek it, purges himself of his own attraction to it, for as Kenneth Burke argues, the satirist simultaneously gratifies and punishes himself by attacking *"in others* the weaknesses and temptations that are really *within himself."*[13] Thus Adams's rejection of power by becoming a historian of his era represents, at the same time, his way of exercising the power that belongs to him by heredity to influence his age, to become a figure in history, and to shape the future.

Adams succeeded in weaving a "web of deception" around his age, and he was able to exercise such power by making his rejection of political power the basis of his rhetoric and method. By presenting himself as alienated from political power, he could become historically real to the very people to whom he had to appeal in order to shape his age in retrospect. And historians have, in fact, found Adams convincing, for they too feel alienated from power, even while they believe themselves to be more capable and more deserving than the people in power. Yet Adams's image of himself as a moth around power becomes more than rhetoric in the figure of the archetypal historian on the steps of Santa Maria d'Ara Coeli. In this pose, Adams comes to share something of Hamlet's graveyard vision of the Caesars and Alexanders and becomes, indeed, an "insect." If political power is vanity, however, Adams sees in literature another means of having power, and achieving power by studying it becomes his paradoxical method. By presenting himself as dwarfed by forces beyond his control, he places himself in the context of the current movements of realism and naturalism and makes of his hero a "realistic" character. Adams, then, wrote his own play for his particular audience; like Hamlet's, his play was a ruse for speaking without speaking, for acting while remaining detached, and for exercising power while rejecting it.

The character of Hamlet may serve as a model for the hero of the *Education* in still other ways. The theme of *Hamlet*, G. Wilson Knight writes, is death—life bound for disintegration.[14] Knight's observation that Hamlet is "the ambassador of death walking amid life" is corroborated by James Kirsch in his psychoanalytic study of the play. In his view, Ophelia's drowning symbolizes the death of Hamlet's soul,[15] and without his anima Hamlet is "dead" long before the final scene. Likewise, it may be argued that the theme of the *Education* is decay, dissipation, and death— not only of the protagonist but of his society. Social change is seen as disintegration, which parallels Adams's own "decay": "He had hugged his antiquated dislike of bankers and capitalistic society until he had become little better than a crank. He had known for years that he must accept the régime, but he had known a great many other disagreeable certainties—like age, senility, and death—against which one made what little resistance one could" (pp. 343– 344). The question, however, was what form the resistance should take, since mere "readiness" for death would not suffice: ". . . the affectation of readiness for death is a stage rôle, and stoicism is a stupid resource, though the only one. . . . One is ashamed of it even in the acting" (pp. 395–396).

The ultimate strategy of resistance turned out to be suicidal, for as Thoreau knew before Adams, one can control the future only through anticipation. In order to resist death, then, Adams anticipates it and claims that he is already dead. In the *Education* he considers his life "from

the moment he was born to the moment he died" (p. 4),
and the years after 1890 become the "after life." Adams
writes, for example, that "in Paris and London he had seen
nothing to make a return to life worth while; in Washington he saw plenty of reasons for staying dead" (p. 320).
He develops the same conceit in his private correspondence; for instance, he writes to Elizabeth Cameron that
he is "dead to the world;—dead as Adam and Eve, only
just not yet buried."[16] The consistency of this pose, especially in his correspondence, suggests that it was more than
a literary affectation and that, as repetition-in-reverse, anticipation was indeed a defense—his strategy for control.
Although his habit of portraying himself as dead might
have been based on a feeling, after his wife's suicide, of
being "dead," it eventually became a way of structuring his
experience not only for the *Education* but for the purposes
of being one up on time, his most relentless enemy.

Anticipation is another expression of Adams's essentially
futuristic orientation, which consists, paradoxically, of a
sense of belonging entirely to the past. The *Education* has
its roots in the past and projects itself into the future, but
it leaves a curious vacuum for the present. In the first
chapter, Adams establishes his hero's roots through references not only to the troglodytic and glacial ages, Eve,
Adam, Cain, and Abel but to Saint Augustine, the colonial
period, and the Puritans. In his conclusion, however,
Adams is already in the future, and his speculation about
the possibility of his return to life functions like Whitman's
parting words in "Song of Myself"—"look for me under
your boot-soles." Since Adams calls himself "the runaway
star Groombridge, 1838" (p. 472), his projection of a possible return in 1938 is not entirely fanciful, for the comet
imagery has prepared us for it. In any case, by making
himself coexistent with human history, he covers in the
course of the *Education* the history of humanity. In doing
so, he is not so much effacing himself as transcending the
limitations of his particular span of time. Growing into the

past and future, Henry Adams, who was born in 1838 and was to die in 1918, comes to contain history itself and, in becoming universal consciousness, escapes time as speed.

Thus Adams seems to be in flight from the present. J. C. Levenson proposes that Adams's physical travels in the second part of the *Education* represent excursions away from the present into the past or future.[17] Adams could feel more at home in Egypt or in Shropshire, where one's "time-sequences became interchangeable," than in Washington, for "one's instinct abhors time," and in Shropshire "nothing suggested sequence. The Roman road was twin to the railroad. . . . One might mix up the terms of time as one liked, or stuff the present anywhere into the past" (pp. 228–229). In the *Education* as a whole, in fact, the present is absent. Chronologically, there is a gap of twenty years between Adams's eighteenth-century education, which far from preparing him for the future left him closer to "the year 1," and the twentieth-century future, which resists connection to the past and is therefore chaotic. The present, which *is* the connection between the past and the future, remains unrealized, and Adams's education teaches only the breakdown of sequence.

For Adams, not only education but history and life itself "broke in halves." The modern historian could not have Gibbon's faith in sequence and causality, for no law of progress could account for the history of Rome: "Not even time-sequences—the last refuge of helpless historians— had value for it. The Forum no more led to the Vatican than the Vatican to the Forum" (p. 91). There is no more sequence in Adams's own life; since the present is unreal, neither the past nor the future makes sense: ". . . the happiest month of May that life had yet offered, fading behind the present, and probably beyond the past, somewhere into abstract time, grotesquely out of place with the Berlin scheme or a Boston future" (p. 93). Adams's environment comes to reflect and thereby to emphasize the breakdown of sequence in his own life: ". . . he saw before him a world so changed as to be beyond connection with the past.

His identity, if one could call a bundle of disconnected memories an identity, seemed to remain; but his life was once more broken into separate pieces; he was a spider and had to spin a new web in some new place with a new attachment" (p. 209). It is this experience of discontinuity that forced him to keep one jump ahead of the present, for "he was in a fair way to do himself lasting harm, floundering between worlds passed and worlds coming, which had a habit of crushing men who stayed too long at the points of contact" (p. 83). In order to avoid the point of contact, Adams's hero transcends the present and comes to embody both "worlds passed" and "worlds coming," thereby containing the time from the troglodytic age to 1938. Through anticipation and by posing as already dead, he lives as though his life were over—as though the future had bypassed the present entirely and had already become the past.

Adams even shapes autobiography to his particular needs, for autobiography, which may be seen as a strategy of resurrection, becomes in his hands a strategy for suicide as well. Normally, autobiography is an open-ended form; by pretending that his life is over, however, Adams gets around the imperfection that is inherent in his form. Yet if life becomes complete only with death, autobiography that aims at formal wholeness becomes suicidal. Adams explicitly associates autobiography with death; for example, he writes to John Hay in 1883, "I am clear that you should write autobiography. I mean to do mine. After seeing how coolly and neatly a man like Trollope can destroy the last vestige of heroism in his own life, I object to allowing mine to be murdered by any one except myself."[18] On the surface, Adams is contemplating the advantages of what is to become his strategy in the Education; his pose will make it impossible for anyone to write an unfavorable biography of him, since it will have been done, so to speak. The unsettling image of suicide is not accidental, however, for he sounds a similar note in a letter to Henry James in 1908: "The volume [the Education] is a mere shield of protection in the grave. I advise you to take your own life in the same way, in order to prevent biographers from taking it in theirs."[19] It is appropriate, then, that Adams's "life" ends with Hamlet's dying words, "The rest is silence."

Yet Adams is even more ambitious than Thoreau, for he sets out to anticipate not only nature but the course of history. Once again, his attempt to control the future through anticipation leads him to develop a suicidal theory of history. Psychologically, his theory is a way of getting the worst over with. And his theory is necessarily a projection of death, for his *method*, as he well knows, is suicidal: "For human purposes a point must always be soon reached where larger synthesis is suicide" (p. 402). Knowing this fact, he proceeds to formulate larger and larger syntheses: "Adams proclaimed that in the last synthesis, order and anarchy were one, but that the unity was chaos" (p. 406). His method is thus suicidal, because it ultimately leads to the negation of all mental effort, not to speak of the effort to run "order through chaos" by writing autobiography. Moreover, Adams does not simply resign himself to the death to which he has brought himself; instead, he would positively encourage it with a recklessness that is reminiscent of certain Poe narrators: "As anarchist, conservative and Christian, he had no motive or duty but to attain the end; and, to hasten it, he was bound to accelerate progress; to concentrate energy; to accumulate power; to multiply and intensify forces; to reduce friction, increase velocity and magnify momentum, partly because this was the mechanical law of the universe as science explained it; but partly also in order to get done with the present which artists and some others complained of; and finally—and chiefly—because a rigorous philosophy required it, in order to penetrate the beyond, and satisfy man's destiny by reaching the largest synthesis in its ultimate contradiction" (pp. 406–407). In Adams's suicidal system, the largest synthesis is its own ultimate contradiction—death.

In the end, however, Adams's method comes to his rescue, for it is so thoroughly suicidal that it can successfully overturn its own catastrophic vision: "Any student, of any age, thinking only of a thought and not of his thought, should delight in turning about and trying the opposite motion, as he delights in the spring which brings even to a tired and irritated statesman the larger synthesis of peach-blooms, cherry-blossoms, and dogwood, to prove the folly of fret" (p. 402). In this quick shift of perspective, which introduces his sense of "the folly of fret," Adams's hero once again recalls Hamlet, now not as tragic hero but as fool.

In *The Fool and His Scepter*, William Willeford observes that the magic function of the fool, who traditionally accompanied the king, was prevention by anticipation. The fool represented the possibility that the kingly office might lose its power, that the realm beyond the borders of the kingdom might become unruly, and that chaos might come to reign over order. By making these threats present to the imagination, he diminished their possibility. The fool, then, is properly the alter ego of the king and counteracts threats to order by "embodying the principle of wholeness, by reinstating in measured form the primeval condition before the separation of the kingdom from that which it excludes." Although a number of readers have noted Hamlet's affinity to the fool, Willeford's interpretation of this likeness is particularly useful here. According to Willeford, Hamlet is, in a sense, his own fool, for "just as the kingdom lacks an adequate king, so it lacks anyone in whom folly assumes a redeeming form: the hero is not really abetted by his folly, and there is no helpful jester. The ambiguity in the person of the king is reflected in Hamlet's fluctuation between the possibilities of heroism and those of folly." The killing of the "false king" would require a "hero" who could divest himself of his folly and act to legitimate the kingship: Hamlet's uncertainty, however, and his position in the play as a "center of indifference" in the midst of the action make him more a clown than a hero. As a clown, Hamlet can suspend his personal feelings and enjoy the fool's freedom—the freedom of "the mourner who laughs at a funeral." Thus, since Hamlet is wise "in the way the old king should be" but lacks "both the king's position and a jester of his own," he must "stumble in and out of the folly which he tries simultaneously to divest himself of and to enact."[20] As a result, he ends up—in the graveyard scene, for example—joking and moralizing at once, for he feels, in Francis Fergusson's words, "like the gag-man and the royal victim in one."[21]

Adams's position in the *Education* is not unlike Hamlet's, for Adams also plays the fool in his role of detached spectator. He casts himself as the comic center of indifference, who is absorbed in studying the game of life. Adams himself suggests that we may see the *Education* as the story of how he came to occupy the position of the fool. He writes, "The tailor's object, in this volume, is to fit young men, in universities or elsewhere, to be men of the world, equipped for any emergency; and the garment offered to them is meant to show the faults of the patchwork fitted on their fathers" (p. xxiv). Patchwork or motley is, of course, the traditional costume of the fool; it is the disguise of chaos, which the fool stands for.[22] For a man in Adams's position, the role of the fool was quite legitimate. If, as he wrote in a letter to his brother Brooks, pessimism was the only dignified pose for someone with an annual income of less than $50,000,[23] the role of the fool was the only dignified position for a "stable-companion to statesmen" (p. 317), for a moth around power. Thus laughter became the only possible response for Adams. Like Hamlet, Adams's hero is deprived of his legitimate role and hints that his dispossession is partly the cause and symptom of the social decay around him: "Society laughed a vacant and meaningless derision over its own failure. Nothing remained for a young man without position or power except to laugh too" (pp. 272–273). Adams's self-consciousness is as withering as Hamlet's and leaves him in a suicidal position; as the dispossessed heir, he must be hero and fool at the same time, and self-destruction is built into this double role.

Yet we must depart finally from the Hamlet model, for Adams is essentially a comic writer, and the *Education* is best comprehended as a comedy. Since his critics tend to see him as a "heroic failure," the *Education* is generally read as a tragedy.[24] Yet Adams's view of himself as unheroic makes him a typically twentieth-century comic figure.[25] More modern than some of the Moderns, Adams's hero is not the failed hero, who, like Prufrock, is "Almost, at times, the Fool"; instead, he is hero and fool in one. By considering the *Education* as comedy, we can account both for Adams's comic hero—who is a positive character, not the failure of something else—and for the diverse elements of the book, because the perspective of comedy enables us to accept contradiction and even chaos. From this perspective, the chaos that the *Education* embodies appears not as an aberration but as part of its form. For Adams does not create confusion for the sake of wit, as some readers argue;[26] rather, wit, irony, and humor are his devices for dealing not only with the chaos surrounding him but with the corresponding confusion in his mind, which his contradictory interests, loyalties, and desires create.

According to Wylie Sypher, the comical arises from a "sudden perception of incongruity" between man's ideals and actuality. For the "modern hero" lives with "irreconcilables which . . . can be encompassed only by religious faith—or comedy."[27] For Adams, comedy became just such a strategy for dealing with the incongruities of his situation: it became a substitute for the faith that he could not quite muster. In his case, the basic irreconcilables were the dream or nightmare of history as it is lived and the order that the mind craves but only in retrospect achieves. Adams continually refers to the present as an incomprehensible dream—a nightmare: slavery was "a nightmare; a horror" (p. 44); Berlin was "a nightmare" (p. 81); in London, the past was more real than the present (p. 72); and even Nature was "a nightmare, an insanity of force" (p. 288). Since the present became somewhat fantastic, "the chaos of education approached a dream" (p. 467).

For order and purpose exist only in retrospect—not only in the life of the individual but in society as a whole. History as it is being made is, as Maurice Merleau-Ponty has argued, "dream or nightmare"; it becomes real only to future generations.[28]

History is a nightmare because it is riddled with contradictions. From childhood on, Adams learns that "in practice, such trifles as contradictions in principle are easily set aside; the faculty of ignoring them makes the practical man; but any attempt to deal with them seriously as education is fatal" (p. 48). If it is fatal to beat one's head against such contradictions, it is also fatal to transcend them, and the choice of the comic hero is, in its way, also suicidal, because it is destructive of reality. The comic hero accepts the incompatibles in reality in the act of transcending them by a "perspective from infinity"; from this perspective, however, life appears as a dream. Whereas from the perspective within history the present is a nightmare, from the point of view of the infinite the present is surreal—a comic dream in which the individual appears pathetically powerless.

What is distinctive about the *Education*, however, is that it is an autobiography: it is Adams himself who provides his life with a perspective from infinity. And from this perspective, "one cannot take one's self quite seriously," for "it could not much affect the sum of solar energies whether one went on dancing with girls in Washington, or began talking to boys at Cambridge" (p. 293). From this point of view, then, "Henry's adventures in search of an education . . . tended to humor" (p. 116). If, in comedy, a perspective from within history and a perspective from outside history coexist, the *Education* may be seen as a comic drama. Since it is an autobiography, however, both these perspectives are supplied by Adams himself, and the force that makes his hero into a manikin or little man is actually the power of Adams's mind. It is the mind that is vast, and the mind's conception of the absolute is the absolute. In relation to the mind, one's self in history is seen as insignificant and comic. Ultimately, it is Adams's theory of history that renders his hero's trials absurd, for the theory provides a perspective from infinity by reducing the universe to mechanism. Thus his hero is necessarily a manikin or puppet acting as in a dream, while Adams—the "philosopher"—works "as though he were a small God and immortal and possibly omniscient."[29]

Once again, Adams's world is a closed system, and his strategy is doubly suicidal, for his theory of history, which reduces him—along with the rest of the human race—to insignificance, is itself the embodiment of the suicidal nature of his mind. Adams writes to Elizabeth Cameron in 1911 that William Bigelow and he "agreed that the whole thing must be an illusion, and that our world was a mere dream, reflecting our minds as they grew to their end. The whole show will suddenly vanish some day when I get a stroke. Good thing too!"[30] In a somewhat different tone, he writes to Charles Francis Adams: "I can't see how the thing can possibly run. . . . We can't go forward to a perpetual deadlock. It is an amusing jig-saw puzzle; to me, the more amusing because I tried to state it some five years ago in my volume on *Education*, and the crisis has come five years earlier than I expected. I can add nothing to what I said then, which was, in substance, that I know I'm a damn fool, and my folly ends in the logical and mathematical demonstration that the human race is going to end just when I do."[31] As the *Education* makes clear, if Henry Adams is a "runaway star," so is the earth itself. This kind of rhetoric partly represents Adams's comic revenge on the world, since "a world which cannot educate, will not amuse, and is ugly besides, has even less right to exist than he" (p. 357). So he decides to blow it up! More important, his destructiveness is an expression of his solipsism. According to Freud, catastrophic visions that project the end of the world are symptomatic of paranoia or the withdrawal of libidinal instincts from the world. This narcissistic state, Freud adds, is often seen in people who are in mourning.[32] In Adams's case, it was in the essentially narcissistic act of writing autobiography or self-history that history itself became equated with the self's story. As a result, the strategy of controlling one's fate through anticipation grew logically into an anticipation of the end of human history itself.

Unlike Thoreau, Whitman, and James, all of whom regard their lives in historical time from the vantage point of consciousness, Adams internalizes the perspective of history and considers his consciousness from the vantage point of various histories—from world history and evolution to the American heritage and the tradition of autobiography. For him, therefore, time is not a self-renewing, inner experience; instead, it is speed—it is clocks ticking away. Since Adams is concerned with entropy in various forms, Hamlet's perspective in the graveyard scene is built into the *Education*. The double perspective that structures the chronology of the *Education* enables Adams to view himself from the distance of two centuries. As an eighteenth-century hero, he embarks on an eighteenth-century picaresque journey of initiation in the ways of the world. With his firm sense of what is good and real, Adams starts out *in* the eighteenth century, periodically even reverts— as he admits—to the seventeenth, and, with the systematic destruction of such certainties, ends up in the twentieth. All the old certainties dissolve in illusion or politics, which may come to the same thing. Adams presents his progress from certainty to confusion as a journey through two centuries, which also happen to encompass all American history. He not only wrote—along with John Hay—"nearly all the American history there was" (p. 325) but became that history, and if he was weak in the nineteenth century, Hay could cover for him nicely. Accordingly, since Adams does not judge himself in the light of his consciousness, his so-called failure becomes part of a universal failure, not a personal shortcoming, for taking a cosmic perspective allows him to bypass the issue of personal success or failure. Thus his theory of history, which has seemed to some readers too visionary and somewhat irresponsible as history, is primarily a literary strategy.

True to his method of self-contradiction, Adams proceeds to undercut even his theory, for the person who so ambitiously charts the history of human civilization in some fifteen pages is, after all, only an insect—exactly what his theory reduces him to. Charles Vandersee studies the animal imagery in Adams but does not remark that Adams reserves the numerous insect images primarily for himself.[33] For example, to the "Concord Church" he remained "always an insect" (p. 63), and to Swinburne he was merely an "American insect" (p. 143). As the *Education* progresses, the tone of such images becomes increasingly ambiguous. The "private secretary"—"a young mosquito" (p. 103)—wanders around in society "like a maggot in cheese" (p. 197), only to become in later years a "gray-headed moth" that flutters around power in Washington (p. 417). In the transformations of the insect imagery, we witness Adams's development of a truly double-edged irony. He also keeps his distance from his theory through such offhand qualifications as, for example, "the dynamic scheme began by asserting rather recklessly . . ." (p. 482) and "this, then, or something like this, would be a dynamic formula of history" (p. 487).

Adams would have to disclaim his theory, inasmuch as "since the time of Socrates, wise men have been mostly shy of claiming to understand anything" (p. 407). Yet he dissociates himself from Socrates in the very act of invoking him. As Adams knows, unless one takes an ironic attitude toward oneself *as* ironist, one's irony—even if it is self-irony—leaves one vulnerable. Since irony implies a consciousness of superiority, it leaves the ironist vulnerable to irony from a higher level than one's own.[34] Thus only a Socrates who can take an ironic attitude toward the "wisdom" of his own ironic method is totally protected, and Adams shows this kind of circumspection, because the *irony* of his suggestion that he is as "wise" as Socrates

precludes our questioning his wisdom and thereby proves—
ironically?—his "wisdom." Since his self-referring method
is not Socratic but Romantic irony, he is protected not only
from the world but from himself. Romantic irony, which
involves an awareness of the potentially infinitely regressive nature of irony, protects authors from being limited
by their own work.[35] Being self-conscious about one's
strategy, then, is self-protective precisely because it is self-
destructive. It is Adams's attitude toward the reworked
version of his theory of history that most clearly illustrates
his method. He writes to Elizabeth Cameron, "I'm amusing
myself by printing a little volume to make fun of my fellow
historians. The fun of it is that not one of them will understand the fun." Yet this irony toward himself as historian
is transcended by his irony toward himself as ironist: "I
don't know that I should see the joke myself if I were not
its author." The joke, however, is not wholly on himself,
for having achieved this degree of self-consciousness, he
can safely be an ironist: "Luckily nothing matters, and no
one cares. America is a vast mud-flat; you can pepper it
with stones but they all disappear instantly without a
splash."[36]

Like his comic perspective, Adams's irony enabled him
to confront his life by cutting it down to size. Since humor
helps us survive our difficulties by belittling them, we could
say that humor enabled Adams to survive Henry Adams by
making light of him. Indeed, humor is the one lesson that
education teaches; as truth evaporates, all that remains is
amusement: "Henry Adams was the first in an infinite
series to discover and admit to himself that he really did
not care whether truth was, or was not, true. He did not
even care that it should be proved true, unless the process
were new and amusing. He was a Darwinian for fun" (pp.
231–232). As for education itself, "he cared not whether
it were worth finishing, if only it amused" (p. 338). Yet his
criterion for education is not at all frivolous. We have seen
that in Freud's terms laughter is a way of economizing on
the expenditure of psychic energy. Thus education, the ob-

ject of which was to enable the mind "to react with vigor and economy," could at best teach laughter, for Adams knew with Carlyle that it is "thriftless work" for a person to complain of "his 'element,' of his 'time,' or the like."[37] Adams did see too much even into himself, and comedy's double perspective made it possible for him to live with his contradictions by enabling him simultaneously to justify *and* to judge the life of his hero. As comic author, then, Adams not only escapes being defined by his "mortal" hero but avoids being contained within his book.

The point of view in autobiographical writing in general may be seen as essentially comic. To begin with, self-consciousness is the basis of the comic—from the lowest form of humor, which arises from self-consciousness about the body, to the most sophisticated wit, which indicates a society's self-consciousness about its opinions, etiquette, and manners. Similarly, self-consciousness is basic to autobiography and accounts for the double perspective of the *Education*, which tells, in a sense, two life stories. Stephen Spender discusses the doubleness that informs autobiography: ". . . unless one is to oneself entirely public, it seems that the problem of an autobiographer, when he considers the material of his own past, is that he is confronted not by one life—which he sees from the outside—but by two. One of these lives is himself as others see him—his social or historic personality . . . [which is] real to him as, say, his own image in a mirror. But there is also himself known only to himself, himself seen from the inside of his own existence." This inside self has a history of its own—"the history of himself observing the observer, and not as the observed of others."[38] Accordingly, although the *Education* is ostensibly the history of Adams's public self, both the shape of the book and the narrator's attitudes and language, which reflect the author's aims and strategies, tell a private story. Thus the public story transpires within the structures of the private story, while the private history is shaped as a response to the public history.

Furthermore, it is only the fate of the tragic hero that must be made to appear intelligible or at least inevitable. In the essentially self-conscious act of writing one's life, however, one would realize— even while attempting to render one's past inevitable—that one's fate need not be made intelligible to anyone but oneself and that the recording of one's life is ultimately as unjustifiable as the life would be without the recording. As we move into modern autobiographical writing, this self-doubt becomes more menacing. Henry James recollecting his career in the Prefaces is a transitional figure: whereas, like Whitman, he never lets himself seriously doubt the importance of his task, he also feels obliged to excuse his account as "lucubrations" interesting to no one but the fatuous author, and he takes care to write a final Preface justifying the entire project. For Adams, the doubts are more serious, and the self-assertion is correspondingly more desperate. On the one hand, Adams's megalomania—his sense that his consciousness is life itself—leads him to see his death as the end of the world; on the other hand, his comic perspective —which arises precisely from the magnitude of his intellectual ambitions—will not let him forget that he is, indeed, an insect. Moreover, the retrospective point of view in autobiography contributes to the diminution of the hero, since from the point of view of the older self and his "wisdom" and "humility," the younger self floundering in the nightmare of history appears to be somewhat comic. In other words, looking at his life from the inside, Adams is a tragic writer trying to make his fate intelligible in relation to the universe, and he is, in fact, looking at himself from the inside, since he is writing autobiography. Looking at himself from the outside, however, he knows that his fate need not be intelligible, and as the distance of his third-person narration attests, he is also looking at himself from the outside. The third-person pronoun is ambiguous, for it inflates the hero Henry Adams by building up our expectations of him while at the same time deflating him as a source of power. As consciousness, the "I" is always a creative power, but a "he" can easily become a puppet of the forces that the "I" envisions as acting upon it.

Considering the *Education* as comedy enables us to account for a number of its dominant patterns. To regard Adams's basic impulse as suicidal would seem to suggest that the *Education* fits the pattern of tragedy; to insist that the work is a comedy, however, is to assert that it transcends the tragic pattern of birth, growth, and death and enters a new life cycle by affirming continuity through rebirth. In fact, rebirth is a recurrent pattern throughout the *Education*, for education itself is a process of continual transformation: when a boy's will is broken, Adams writes of the first chapter of his education, "he dies." Afterward, he is no longer a boy, or at least he is not the same boy. Education, then, represents the death of one identity and the subsequent birth of another. Moreover, a number of "deaths" in the *Education* are accompanied by images of rebirth. Adams is already reborn before he is even four: "On December 3, 1841, he developed scarlet fever. For several days he was as good as dead, reviving only under the careful nursing of his family" (p. 5). The crucial death in the *Education* is, of course, the death of his sister, which constitutes "the last lesson—the sum and term of education" (p. 287) and teaches Adams that death is the "larger synthesis." Once more his will is broken, and he devotes the rest of his career to anticipating and even hastening death. "He had never seen Nature—only her surface," Adams writes. "Flung suddenly in his face, with the harsh brutality of chance, the terror of the blow stayed by him thenceforth for life, until repetition made it more than the will could struggle with; more than he could call on himself to bear" (p. 287). Thus his sister's death comes to represent not only the unmentioned death of his wife but his own "death," for as we have seen Adams "dies" before the second part of the *Education*. In this view, the second part may be considered a rebirth; as Robert Sayre remarks, the opening pages of "Twenty Years After" abound with images of "change and renewal," because Adams returns as a different man to a changed world.[39] The structure of the *Education*, then, affirms a rebirth, for the relation between its two movements cannot be called a continuity: "Life had been cut in halves," Adams writes, "and the old half had passed away, education and all, leaving no stock to graft on" (p. 317). After running "down hill, for twenty years, into the bog labelled Failure," education has to begin anew "to crawl uphill a little way."[40]

The writing of autobiography is itself a form of resurrection. Before one begins an autobiography, or at least some time before one is through, one's life must have reached the point at which the autobiography is to end. In a sense, then, after Hamlet's "The rest is silence," Adams has to return as his own Horatio to carry out Hamlet's last request:

> Absent thee from felicity awhile,
> And in this harsh world draw thy breath in pain,
> To tell my story.

Since in autobiography one records one's life after it is over, so to speak, one is reborn in the act of writing. The curiously optimistic lines that conclude the *Education* reaffirm this theme of rebirth and thus make a properly comic ending for Adams's autobiography. As we have seen, the open-ended form of autobiography was too messy for him, and knowing that death was the "larger synthesis" even of his form, he resorted to playing dead in order to give a formal wholeness to what was in any case "self-murder." Still, the *Education* closes with Adams's suggesting the possibility of his rebirth, and the unexpected change of tone in the concluding sentences contributes to the comic effect of the ending: "Perhaps some day—say 1938, their centenary—they might be allowed to return together for a holiday, to see the mistakes of their own lives made clear in the light of the mistakes of their successors; and perhaps then, for the first time since man began his education among the carnivores, they would find a world that sensitive and timid natures could regard without a shudder" (p. 505). Adams knows that he is writing comedy, and he manages—if somewhat sheepishly—to surface finally, to affirm the continuity of society, and even to project its regeneration.

Approaching the *Education* as comedy enables us to account not only for its form and structure but for its social scope as well. According to Francis Cornford, whereas tragedy reflects the human destiny or "the turning wheel of Time and Fate," comedy mirrors contemporary society, and Hamlet's instructions to his players serve well as a definition of comedy: it shows "virtue her own feature, scorn her own image, and the very age and body of the time his form and pressure." Comedy, then, is "no magic mirror"; reflecting the present time and place, it is closer to history than to myth. Yet as "a permanent possibility of human nature, independent of its accidental trappings of time and country," the comic hero is at the same time more universal.[41] Accordingly, although the *Education* is a reflection of its historical time and place, Adams is able to make his hero into the universal Seeker or Wanderer. Comedy was particularly well suited to his purposes, for like Dante—to whom Adams compares himself—he was writing about a particular society in which he had personal stakes as well as personal scores to settle. It was the largeness of comedy, then, that allowed Adams to be personal and impersonal at once and enabled him to write *his* autobiography "in colossal cipher."

Moreover, Adams's social and political views found in comedy their most congenial form of expression. His almost wholesale rejection of contemporary society approaches what Kenneth Burke describes as the typical debunker's policy: the debunker is essentially suicidal, for in rejecting everything one also rejects a frame of acceptance, which alone could make one's rejection intelligible —if less than wholesale.[42] Adams's rejection is nearly as absolute. Although he denounces nineteenth-century America for abandoning certain eighteenth-century practices and ideals, he himself criticizes the same ideals as outmoded, for he lacks the value system that supported them; for example, he does not have the eighteenth century's optimism and faith in reason. Once again, then, Adams is both in and out of the game, and Fergusson's statement about Hamlet could characterize Adams: "His intellect plays over the world of the religious tradition with an all-dissolving irony . . . , for he can neither do with nor do without the ancient moral and cosmic order."[43] Although Adams criticizes the present, he lacks a frame of acceptance within which to judge it; he cannot bring himself to say, for instance, that capitalism has failed or that democracy is unworkable. Thus his criticism becomes ineffectual and serves essentially the purpose of upholding things as they are.

Since Adams makes chaos his very form and subject, however, no proof is needed that the *Education* is also the work of an anarchist. For anarchism is the other side of Adams's kind of conservatism, and his description of himself as a conservative anarchist is indeed accurate. This anomalous position defines a comic perspective, since comedy is at once socially conservative and radical: "The ambivalence of comedy reappears in its social meanings, for comedy is both hatred and revel, rebellion and defense, attack and escape. It is revolutionary and conservative." By laughing at evil and error, the comedian releases us from the limits of the actual. In this role, the comedian is a conservative, for comedy serves to uphold the system by enabling us to live with it. Yet the comedian also represents a "permanent resistance movement," for comedy in fact makes fewer concessions to actuality—to things as they are—than tragedy.[44] We could say, then, that as a conservative anarchist Adams was playing the comedian. And this role enabled him to live with his contradictions, not by tackling them morally as a tragic hero might but by learning to accept them in the very act of resisting them.

Adams's projected title—"The Education of Henry Adams: A Study in Twentieth-Century Multiplicity"—sug-

gests that he attempted partly to make his life a historical
or space-time event. Yet it is idle to argue that the *Education* is not an autobiography, for whether we choose to approach it as history or as literature, the experience that informs its subject, statement, and style remains personal.
Indeed, because it is an autobiography—because it *is* the
synthesis of the person and the age—the *Education* presents us with a variety of Henry Adamses. First, Adams is
any person in history. As such, he not only responds to
his particular time but reacts to the fact of life in time—
his mortality. The *Education*, then, should be seen as a
gesture or a strategy for living; it embodies the contradictions in his experience, achieves mastery over the past
through repetition, and resists the "undiscover'd" future
through anticipation. Second, Adams keeps reminding us
that he is also an Adams in history, and as such he is committed to certain social and political standards and necessarily judges his time. Thus the *Education* is also rhetoric,
and as conscious rhetoric it is addressed to two different
audiences. Adams is immediately speaking for the small
group of the elect to whom he sent copies of the *Education*;
at the same time, however, he is speaking to the hordes
of the vulgar, who will come one day to read him. As a result, although his style has a distinctly public manner, it
also has a private edge, which complicates the irony and
makes the reader of today conscious of reading a somewhat
different book than the one read, say, by Brooks Adams.
Third, Adams is a historian creating *his* time, and the *Education* is a historical document. Since in this role he is addressing historians of the future, his alienation from political power becomes a full-fledged rhetoric of failure that
aims to appeal to an equally powerless audience. Finally,
Adams is an artist, and the *Education* is, in his words to
William James, "a literary experiment" of the kind "your
brother Harry tries . . . daily."[45] As a "literary experiment,"
it has a necessity of its own: ". . . the pen becomes a sort
of blind-man's dog, to keep him from falling into the gut-
ters. The pen works for itself, and acts like a hand, model-

ling the plastic material over and over again to the form that suits it best. The form is never arbitrary, but is a sort of growth like crystallization, as any artist knows too well" (p. 389).

These distinctions are a luxury that we can afford only in retrospect, for the peculiarly explosive form of the *Education* derives from the fact that Adams's roles are not distinct but blend together, interact, and even conflict. He writes: "St. Augustine, like a great artist, had worked from multiplicity to unity, while he, like a small one, had to reverse the method and work back from unity to multiplicity. The scheme became unmanageable as he approached his end" (p. xxi). Adams's mock modesty notwithstanding, this statement accurately describes the *Education*, for he knows that his book is suicidal. Since his search for education becomes almost a search for the secret of life itself, he seems at times to be chasing another white whale. Yet he himself counters his lust for order with the awareness that moves Emily Dickinson to lament:

Alas, that Wisdom is so large—
And Truth—so manifold![46]

As a result, Adams necessarily adopts the stance and the tone of Wallace Stevens's "Connoisseur of Chaos":

A. A violent order is disorder; and
B. A great disorder is an order. These
Two things are one. (Pages of illustrations.)[47]

We could even say that the project of the *Education* itself forced Adams to undertake his search for order. The *Education* created the very need for order that it portrays, for to write autobiography Adams had to discover a principle that would justify his personal history by relating it to American history, world history, the state of scientific knowledge, and the evolution of the species. Accordingly, the law of increasing multiplicity, which became his principle for uniting diverse phenomena and even determined the structure of the *Education*, has psychological truth as

well; for example, childhood comes to stand for unity, because one can remember only so much of it. Likewise, the
law of acceleration of disintegration, which informs the
frenzied second movement of the *Education*, reflects the
psychological phenomenon that time goes faster the older
one grows. The *Education* is successful, then, because
Adams's theories admit of being read as metaphors and
thereby serve, in fact, to establish connections between
the narrative and the didacticism. Reading his theories in
any other terms would amount to judging the *Education*
as more or less incoherent.

"Every man," Adams writes, "with self-respect enough to
become effective, if only as a machine, has had to account
to himself for himself somehow, and to invent a formula
of his own for his universe, if the standard formulas failed"
(p. 472). Adams suggests, however, that not only the formulas but the very means of their invention failed: perhaps "art [was] fragmentary by essence. History, like everything else, might be a field of scraps" (p. 221). In such
straits, he could not be sure even of himself as a continuous and real entity. Adams continually doubts his own
reality, and his use of the third person in his autobiography
reflects his idea of personality as disconnected and unse-
quential. From his point of view, it was only the doubting
self—the self as author—that could be trusted. Thus the
lessons or nonlessons of his continuing education served
only to justify his project of comic autobiography. Since he
could avoid the falseness of imposed orders only by accept-
ing disorder as the basis even of his form, he could only
write comedy, which alone allows for disorder in art. Similarly, since only the doubter recording his doubts was real,
Adams could only write autobiography.

Chapter 5
Two Poets

The anti-poetic has many aspects. The aspect to which a poet is addicted is a test of his validity. Its merely rhetorical aspect is valueless. As an affectation it is a commonplace. As a scourge it has a little more meaning. But as a phase of a man's spirit, as a source of salvation, now, in the midst of a baffled generation, as one looks out of the window at Rutherford or Passaic, or as one walks the streets of New York, the anti-poetic acquires an extraordinary potency, especially if one's nature possesses that side so attractive to the furies.

—WALLACE STEVENS

If the consciousness of a major split between life and art or between history and form underlies the nineteenth-century autobiographical writer's urge to infuse history with form, the same consciousness accounts for the twentieth-century transformations of autobiographical writing. Only the emphasis shifts, and the twentieth-century writer, more aware of the arbitrariness of form, tries in fact to infuse form with history. The problem that the poets William Carlos Williams and Frank O'Hara face is not so much how to order history so that it may partake of the necessity of a formal existence but how to guard the historical nature of their experience—its everydayness— from the false finishes and impersonal orders of form. This impulse leads, of course, not to less self-consciousness but to an increased consciousness of style, because everyday life as subject matter demands a technically innovative art. In his discussion of realism, Wylie Sypher points out that the realists' attempt to be "banal" led to a heightened awareness of style, for the "realists wished to present the expected, the banal; but the really banal painting was academic—that is, in the 'classic' tradition."[1] Williams's and O'Hara's desire to incorporate everyday life in their art drove them also to technical innovation, since they too had to break away from the banal-academic in order to capture the banal-quotidian. Since the banal-quotidian or everyday life is—as Henri Lefebvre, for example, insists—a specifically modern phenomenon, it must be discovered in an appropriately new language. Such a discovery would amount to a transformation, which would render the quotidian accessible to art. Everyday life, then, can be transformed only *through* itself, and the writer's task is not to disown or evade the quotidian in languages foreign to it but to discover and embrace it in a new language, so that everyday life will assume its place as the creative basis of modern life.[2] For as Wallace Stevens's "comedian" comes to realize:

> . . . the quotidian
> Like this, saps like the sun, true fortuner.
> For all it takes it gives a humped return
> Exchequering from piebald fiscs unkeyed.[3]

The trick is to make the quotidian "give" and to recognize what it is giving as the gift that it can be.

Among twentieth-century American autobiographical poets, William Carlos Williams and Frank O'Hara were acutely aware of the demands that the banal-quotidian makes on the poet, and they succeeded in discovering a new language of the quotidian, which could transform the banal into something real and special. Williams, for example, announces in *Paterson*:

> Escape from it—but not by running
> away. Not by "composition." Embrace the
> foulness[4]

Here Williams could be speaking for O'Hara as well, and both poets were able to create a new language of the quotidian, because with them the affirmation of the antipoetic was not an affectation. Both wrote a truly personal or autobiographical poetry that came out of and belonged to the overwhelming quotidian around them, and their art has seriousness and urgency because each poet created in his poems the modern environment and himself as a modern man and poet. Their writing has nothing to do with posing; coexistent with living, it is a form of action and affirms grandly that art creates and sustains life itself. O'Hara writes, "I am mainly preoccupied with the world as I experience it, and at times when I would rather be dead the thought that I could never write another poem has so far stopped me."[5] And Williams asks:

> ... Why have I not
> but for imagined beauty where there is none
> or none available, long since
> put myself deliberately in the way of death? (P. 20)

When the need to write is a necessity of life itself, one cannot sit back and "compose" poems. One lives and writes poems in the same act of participating in the present world. The innovative and frankly personal poetry that results is—much like Action Painting according to Harold Rosenberg—"of the same metaphysical substance as the artist's existence."[6] Thus the poetry and the life are *in principle* inseparable, and it is this fusion that energizes both. In re-creating itself in an urgency of life and death, poetry cannot be a craft, and the quotidian, clarified by a language, is no longer destructive.

Paterson: Notes toward an American Revolution

Throughout his career William Carlos Williams maintained that poetry must be integrated with the social life surrounding the poet. According to Williams, if poets in their "fatuous dreams" cut themselves off from society—from "that supplying female"—they dry up their "sources."[7] Williams conceives the relationship between the poet and society as one of reciprocal regeneration. Yet one can be a "social regenerator" only if one is not exclusive in defining the poetic and if this inclusiveness leads to *technical* innovations: "The artist, an individual, a worker, the type of a person who is creative, who has something to give to society must admit all classes of subject to his attention—

even though he hang for it. This is his work. Nothing poetic in the feudal, aristocratic sense but a breaking down, rather of those imposed tyrannies over his verse forms. Technical matters, certainly, but most important to an understanding of the poet as a social regenerator."[8] Society, in turn, regenerates the poet, for the poet derives the new and regenerating forms from the surrounding social life. Against Pound's notion that mind "fertilizes" mind, Williams proposes that "there may be another literary source continuing the greatness of the past which does not develop androgynetically from the past itself mind to mind but from the present, from the hurley-burley of political encounters which determine or may determine it, direct." Thus, Williams urges, "we must acknowledge to ourselves that the origin of the new *is* society, that each society not only originates but fertilizes its whole life, of a piece."[9] In other words, society—or the nonpoetic life—regenerates the poetic life, and the poet regenerates society. Williams thus ends up with a dialectical process of interaction between the poet and the social-political-economic environment or between the poetic and the nonpoetic, art and nonart.

In this way Williams arrives at a revolutionary position not only on art but on society. If society renews art, a new art will, in turn, renew social life. "Who shall tell [the poet] how or what he must write?" Williams asks, for "his very function as a servant of society presupposes his ability to see clearly beyond the formulations of his day and to crystallize his findings in a durable form for social confirmation, that society may be built more praiseworthily.

"He will be the critic of government whether the party in power like it or not.

"The process is ancient and dynamic—that is to say, constantly operative under all conditions. All the best has been maintained in spite of government as a limiting power" (*SE*, p.194). Or as Williams puts it in *Paterson*, "beauty is / a defiance of authority" (p. 119). In his formulation of the dialectical relationship between art and society, then, renewal or the production of novelty becomes a value. It was Williams's association with the Cubists in New York around 1913 that initially helped convince him of the value of novelty. He remembers asking Walter Arensberg what "the more modern painters" like Gleizes, Man Ray, Demuth, and Duchamp were "about". Arensberg replied by saying that "the only way man differed from every other creature was in his ability to improvise novelty and . . . anything in paint that is truly new, truly a fresh creation, is good art" (SE, p. 5). When the improvisation of novelty is seen as a basic human quality, novelty necessarily becomes a value, not only in art but in social life, and Williams is able ultimately to make such a sweeping statement as "nothing is good save the new" (SE, p. 21).

Since novelty alone has value, Williams's only clear social statement is that society must continually change: "The mutability of the truth, Ibsen said it. Jefferson said it. We should have a revolution of some sort in America every ten years" (SE, p. 217). Thus, although Williams was distinctly sympathetic to the aims of communism,[10] he would not become a party member, because communism had already become incorporated as a state and was, therefore, hostile to change. Rather, in positing change as value he places himself in the mainstream of American revolutionary thought. For from Jefferson's call for a revolution in every generation to Emerson's idea of all change as good, a belief in the value of the new constitutes an American tradition of sorts. And art as a social regenerator plays an important role in this projected periodic change; in fact, it is revolutionary art that triggers social change: "How will the artist show the side he has taken? as a man? By subjecting himself, like Lorca, to attack—to be dragged gutless through Granada and burned with his books on the public square? Or to be an exile like Thomas Mann?

"All I say is that, unless all this is already in his writing —in the materials and structure of it—he might better have been a cowhand. The effect of the aristocratic revolution that the artist knows is necessary and intended—must be in his work, in the structure of his work. . . . There has to be new poetry. But the thing is that the change, the greater material, the altered structure of the inevitable revolution must be *in* the poem, in it. Made of it. It must shine in the structural body of it" (*SE*, pp. 216–217). Revolutionary art, then, is not possible within the reactionary structures that are handed down from the past; only aesthetically revolutionary art is also socially revolutionary. Thus a truly new art that can regenerate society is technically innovative—to the point of being "aristocratic"— and revolutionary in its structure. Such art would be analogous to a revolutionary government, for a revolutionary government, which at its best would be nongovernment, would incorporate its antithesis—the process of change— in its structure. Williams, therefore, would see the technical preoccupation of avant-garde art not as a symptom of the sickness of the Western psyche but as a healthy sign pointing to a capacity for change and renewal.[11] For the interrelated changes of the mind, the world, and the poetic line are in fact signs of life:

> Without invention nothing is well spaced,
> unless the mind change, unless
> the stars are new measured, according
> to their relative positions, the
> line will not change, the necessity
> will not matriculate: unless there is
> a new mind there cannot be a new
> line, the old will go on
> repeating itself with recurring
> deadliness: . . .
>
> .   .   .   .
>
> . . . without invention the line
> will never again take on its ancient
> divisions when the word, a supple word,
> lived in it, crumbled now to chalk. (P. 50)

Williams's belief in the value of newness and change enabled him to see not only social life but art in terms of process, and his thoroughly historical view of both society and art precluded separating art from morals or politics. Roland Barthes laments that all too often the avant-garde artist—who opposes the bourgeois in art and morals—remains indifferent or even attached to bourgeois politics, while the political adversary of the bourgeoisie does not condemn its artistic representations and comes even to share them.[12] Williams's avant-gardism, however, was socially responsible because it was responsive to social life. And if his avant-garde art is consciously historical, the phenomenon of the avant-garde is itself a product of the modern historical consciousness. Harold Rosenberg writes that avant-gardism is an attitude based on a "constant awareness of the birth, blending together, and passing away of creatures, styles, values." The qualities of such art—"the freshness of new forms, the estrangement of the transformed, the blankness of the superseded"—represent a historical perspective. This emphasis on the historical nature of experience links avant-gardism with political radicalism, which may be seen as another product of modern historical consciousness. The political implications of impressionism, the first avant-garde art movement, make just this connection. The impressionists, who insisted on freshness as the supreme aesthetic value, were antifeudal and antibourgeois, "insofar as the bourgeoisie had adopted the cult of the heirloom."[13] The historicism of avant-garde art, then, represents ultimately an economic protest against the ownership of art.

Yet the constant creation of novelty implies the simultaneous destruction of the old, and Williams insists throughout *Paterson* that destruction is in fact central to the process of creation:

> Beautiful thing:
>
> —a dark flame,
> a wind, a flood—counter to all staleness. (P. 100)

In this idea of the "beautiful thing" as "the flame's lover" (p. 123) we see a stylistic similarity between radical art and radical politics, which is as significant as their material and historical connections. Rosenberg writes that the vanguards "have infused into art the passion and momentum of radical politics. Their intellectual do-or-die is among their major contributions; it has restored seriousness to the arts and prevented them from degenerating into mere crafts under the pressure of the industrial age."[14] Williams felt the full force of this pressure, and his response has seriousness because he was able to achieve a militant *style*, which gave his voice urgency without recourse to dogma, systems, or theories.

Williams's culturally radical poetics, in which the supreme reality of history confers value on change and newness both in social systems and in the arts, informs his cultural autobiography *Paterson*, which embodies the new not only in its subject but in its structure. In the dialectical view of change that Williams's concept of the mutually regenerative relationship between art and society posits, both art and social life change by absorbing their opposition. Art changes by incorporating hitherto nonartistic realities, and each truly new work is self-transcending, for it redefines art by changing, expanding, and even vulgarizing the definition of art.[15] In the case of *Paterson*, the nonpoetic provides for Williams's very poetics and informs the poem's subject, structure, and language. Thus *Paterson* may be seen as poetry in the process of self-definition; it redefines poetry itself, because it embodies the vulgarization of poetic subject, language, and structure *and* remains poetry. For Williams's "beautiful thing" is not perfection but life, whose "vulgarity of beauty surpasses all their / perfections!" (p. 119).

To begin with, the vulgarization of subject matter involves moving away from "poetic" subjects to the quotidian as subject, and Williams's subject is the urban industrial environment in all its "nonpoetic" aspects. He does not choose to write about a Brooklyn Bridge or a New York City, which might more easily be seen as heroic, if only in its conception; instead, he chooses Paterson, which points to nothing beyond itself. Moreover, Williams does not

choose to make his "modern" subject heroic through sheer
poetic will power, as Hart Crane does, nor does he back
out of it, as T. S. Eliot does. Rather, he searches for a way
to talk about Paterson on its own terms and as he knows
it: *"I knew* of these things. I had *heard.* I had *taken part*
in some of the incidents that made up the place. I had
heard Billy Sunday: I had *talked* with John Reed: I had in
my hospital experiences *got to know* many of the women"
(italics mine). The difficulty was how to talk about all this
as a poet, for "it called for a poetry such as I did not know."
In other words, the problem became how "to *make* a poem,
fulfilling the requirements of the art, and yet new, in the
sense that in the very lay of the syllables Paterson as Paterson would be discovered."[16] His stance, then, is that of a
self-consciously poeticizing poet facing up to Paterson *as
it is.* And this confrontation itself amounts to a transformation of the art and the place. For his announcement in
Spring and All characterizes the poet of *Paterson* as well:
"I speak for the integrity of the soul and the *greatness* of
life's inanity; the *formality* of its boredom; the *orthodoxy*
of its stupidity" (italics mine).[17]

   The tension in the poem, then, is between Paterson and
poetry or between "everyday life in the modern world" and
the poet's task of reconciling "the people and the stones."
The figure of the city embodies this tension, for the city is
both Paterson and the Dr. Paterson who dreams it up—
both fact and poetic subject, both earth and the human
"speech" that shaped it into a city. And the power of *Paterson* derives from Williams's maintaining the tension between the poet and his subject, so that neither is negated
by the other:

>   . . . the city
> the man, an identity—it can't be
> otherwise—an
> interpenetration, both ways. (P. 3)

The image of modern life in Book 2, for example, is as
chilling as anything in *The Waste Land*; the industrial city,
Williams tells us, reflects the alienation—fostered by Chris-

tianity and capitalism—of its inhabitants from the earth under their feet, from what is near and real. To detach one's imagination from the local and the real and to come to see the earth as the "excrement of some sky" is, he insists, what "destroys" us.[18] Williams, however, does not throw up his hands at this point and take refuge in mysticism. Not only does his vision remain inclusive and enable him to interweave what he hears, sees, and thinks and the "poems" that he writes (pp. 66–76), but he remains grounded in the earth. "That the poet, / . . . should borrow from erudition / . . . (borrowing from those he hates, to his own / disfranchisement)" is indeed a "disgrace" for Williams (p. 80), and his hymn to earth or the giant of the place answers "erudite" poets as well as ministers and capitalists:

> If there is subtlety,
> you are subtle. I beg your indulgence:
> no prayer should cause you anything
> but tears. . . .
>
> . . . .
>
> You also, I am sure, have read
> Frazer's Golden Bough. It does you
> justice—a prayer such as might be made
> by a lover who
> appraises every feature of his bride's
> comeliness, and terror—
>
> . . . .
>
> You are the eternal bride and
> father . . .
>
> . . . .
>
> Why should I move from this place
> where I was born? knowing
> how futile would be the search
> for you in the multiplicity
> of your debacle. . . . (Pp. 74–75)

What makes Williams such an effective voice, then, is that as a poet he does precisely what he asks of his townspeople: he returns to the city and owns up to the social and economic realities of the local present. He knows that "We cannot go to the country / for the country will bring us no peace":

> Though you praise us
> and call to mind the poets
> who sung of our loveliness
> it was long ago!
> long ago! when country people
> would plow and sow with
> flowering minds and pockets
>   at ease—
> if ever this were true.

Once, when people still made their living from the earth, there was drama in country life, and the country might have saved us. But "not now":

> Empty pockets make empty heads.
> Cure it if you can but
> do not believe that we can live
> today in the country[19]

Left with the city, we must learn to regard cities not as abnormal growths but as part of present "nature"—as embodying the dramatic encounter of the human and the natural. We must accept what Santayana's Oliver in *The Last Puritan* cannot: ". . . cities are a second body for the human mind, a second organism, more rational, permanent and decorative than the animal organism of flesh and bone: a work of natural yet moral art" (p. 94).

Book 3, which this quote opens, insists that we must come to know the city as a living organic entity, since our salvation lies in city life.[20] Thus the poet must study the history of Paterson, even while asking himself, "Why do I bother with this / rubbish?" (p. 134). The written history of the city is "rubbish" because it is dead residue when compared with the city. If the written history is dead stuff, however, there is also a living history of the city. For we can regard the city itself as writing—as a text "written" by its population, past and present. The numerous analogies in Book 3 between the city and writing affirm that the present shape of the city *is* its history. Like all living organisms, then, the city embodies its history. And as a living organism, the modern city—the creation of industrialism—has the potential to withstand the destructiveness of technological society, which conceives of time as speed and of history as obsolescence. The living city stands forth as the present reality of its past and upholds the idea of time as a creative force as opposed to the concept of time as destruction.

In the balance between Paterson and poetry that Williams maintains throughout his poem, ideas about the non-poetic environment work equally well as ideas about poetry, and Paterson and *Paterson* are never too far apart. In Book 3, for example, Williams affirms the reality of the present city and defends the act of his writing in the same move. First, he admits the lifelessness of all writing that is historical recording:

> We read: not the flames
> but the ruin left
> by the conflagration
>
> Not the enormous burning
> but the dead (the books
> remaining). . . .
>
> .   .   .   .
>
> Dig in—and you have
>
> a nothing, surrounded by
> a surface, an inverted
> bell resounding, a
>
> white-hot man become
> a book, the emptiness of
> a cavern resounding (P. 123)

As art, however, writing also has the power to transcend history and to counter the passage of time by creating a permanence:

Through this hole
at the bottom of the cavern
of death, the imagination
escapes intact. (P. 212)

This is possible in poetry because a poem lives or embodies its history, which it is still making each time it is read. Because poetry embodies its history in a *temporal* structure, moreover, it is capable of withstanding its own dissipation of energy; as Williams asserts, a poem does not "grow old and rot" but remains sensual. Since anything that does not change "rots," the poem survives as long as it changes (*SE*, pp. 196, 197–198). Writing is "dead" to the extent that it approaches written history and opposes itself to "spontaneous Life." In the historical account that Dr. Paterson is reading, for example, even the fire—which represents the destructive-creative force—remains unreal. And if poetry is to partake of the reality of "spontaneous Life," it must itself become as destructive as the fire. The fire of the city, which is the subject, must become *within* the poem a fire of the "library" as well. The very form of the fire-poem, then, must represent the destruction or "burning" of all past dead writing:

Hell's fire. Fire. Sit your horny ass
down. What's your game? Beat you
at your own game, Fire. Outlast you:
Poet Beats Fire at Its Own Game! . . . (P. 118)

Thus art lives only if it is "careless," spontaneous, and as naturally destructive as life itself:

Beautiful thing

—intertwined with the fire. An identity
surmounting the world, its core—from which
we shrink squirting little hoses of
objection . . . (P. 120)

Accordingly, Williams's prescriptions for the ills both of modern poetry and of modern life are the same. Like *Paterson*, the city can be a "marriage" of people and place:

> What end but love, that stares death in the eye?
> A city, a marriage—that stares death
> in the eye (P. 106)

Similarly, Williams's insistence on localism in poetry has
its counterpart in his demand for urban localism. Given
the wholeness of his thought, this total localism amounts
to a cultural revolution. Such a revolution, heralded by
poets who write to the giant of the place, would not only
provide for "LOCAL control of local purchasing / power"
(p. 185) but would begin at the beginning and teach people to live *in* the world, to

> WALK in the world
>   (you can't see anything
> from a car window, still less
> from a plane, or from the moon!? Come
> off of it.) (P. 213)

Williams's thought here would seem to be revolutionary on
the American model: a poet must first change the hearts
of the people, and then urbanism and political and economic reorganization will naturally follow. Since destruction always accompanies creation in Williams, however,
his vision of change would not necessarily exclude violence.
In any case, his focus on the city enabled him to envision
a cultural revolution involving simultaneous economic and
cultural changes. A localist and inclusive art could lead to
a regeneration of everyday life, since it had itself been gen-
erated by the social life. The sources as well as the aims of
this kind of art, then, are ultimately not aesthetic but social.[21] Choosing the industrial city as the subject of his
poem, Williams came to conceive of the sources and aims
of poetry in primarily social terms. Thus his poetic purpose
in *Paterson* is to minister to the needs of his local parish,
to give his people speech so that the "torrent in their minds"
may not be "foreign to them" (p. 12), and to marry them
to their local environment so that their daily lives may become self-expression or self-creation.

The "vulgarization" of language in *Paterson* is "of a piece" with this kind of cultural regeneration. In its language, *Paterson* moves away from Poetry or Art toward more impersonal cultural utterance, for the vulgarization of language involves the incorporation not only of slang, street talk, everyday expressions, and found language but of prose rhythms and structures and even prose itself. Williams's readers have discussed his use of nonpoetic language and prose in *Paterson* in terms of the then-current art movements, especially Cubism. Bram Dijkstra, who studies the influence of Cubism on Williams's early poetry, asserts that Williams's development from a derivative poet to a radically innovative one is the result of his moving away from literary precedents and inspiration and reformulating his art according to the stylistic concepts of the new painters.[22] Similarly, Jerome Mazzaro, who traces the influence of Cubism on Williams's later poetry, regards his use of prose and poetry "as two different facet-planes" as analogous to the "dimensionality" of analytic Cubism. By the time of *Paterson*, however, Williams had arrived at a poetry closer to synthetic Cubism: ". . . for it was not until he began to incorporate items from newspapers and segments of historical documents and letters that one can say that art space begins to intrude on life space and the collage begins."[23] Thus his incorporation of the world outside art parallels the Cubists' use of newspapers, wallpaper, pieces of cloth, and so on, which also served to transform the art space into life space. In Gertrude Stein's terms, such works wanted to come outside their frames and establish contact with their nonartistic environment.

Mazzaro's interpretation of the significance of Williams's collage method is based on a view of Williams's daily life as embodying the psychic tensions of his being at once doctor and poet. The tension between the doctor and the artist or between life and art in Williams's life is reflected in the conflict between prose and poetry in his work. Mazzaro explains how this conflict is worked out in *Kora in Hell*: "These language experiments [prose and poetry echoing themes], in which the operative mode of a poem becomes its thematic statement, approximate attempts by the poet to devise a style consistent with the mythic patterns of his work, devoid of as much subjectivism as possible, to represent how Williams the desperate, descending hero is also Williams the ascendant, Orphean singer. The mood making the poem is also the poem made."[24] This reading works for *Kora in Hell* by establishing the connection between its style and its subject. Since *Paterson* is not only autobiographical but has an announced cultural subject as well, however, we must look into the cultural-artistic implications of Williams's method. The counterpointing of poetry and found prose represents a dramatic encounter of art and nonart or city art and city life, which are the two aspects of Williams's subject. For he is involved in a conversation both with his historical urban environment and with his art. And it is in the act of juxtaposing poetry and found prose that art and the environment enter into a dialectical relationship. The question now becomes whether art is absorbed into the environment, whether the environment is transformed by the art, or whether both occur at once.

Harold Rosenberg observes that in collage—an expression of an advanced industrial age—art no longer copies nature, as in the classical model, or seeks equivalents to it, as in the Romantic and symbolist ideas of parallel structures; instead, art appropriates the external world on the assumption that it is already changed into art.[25] This is exactly how Williams understood the redefinition of poetry in his own time. He writes, for example, that Pound can effectively incorporate prose in his work because all his material is already "changed in *kind* from other statement" (*SE*, p. 108). Thus the use of prose becomes in fact a poetic device. "All the prose" in *Paterson*, Williams claims, "has primarily the purpose of giving a metrical meaning to or of emphasizing a metrical continuity between all word use. It is *not* an antipoetic device. . . . It *is* that prose and verse are both *writing*, both a matter of the words and an interrelation between words for the purpose of exposition,

or other better defined purpose of *the art*"; consequently,
"poetry does not *have* to be kept away from prose as Mr.
Eliot might insist, it goes *along with* prose and, compan-
ionably."[26] In Williams's method, then, the use of prose
does not define poetry by way of contrast; rather, poetry is
redefined by its tolerance for and ability to incorporate
prose or nonart. Art and its nonart environment, therefore,
transform each other in their encounter in *Paterson*.

In this sense, the use of the collage method implies the
presence of a rather overwhelming environment, and the
collage is understandably a product of urban industrial society, where the difficulty is how to pull such disparate and
"divorced" elements into something "fulfilling the requirements of the art":

. . a mass of detail
to interrelate on a new ground, difficultly;
an assonance, a homologue
                                  triple piled
pulling the disparate together to clarify
and compress (P. 20)

Since divorce is so widespread, any synthesis of the frag-
ments—if such a synthesis is possible at all—has to be
more than literary, and Williams's collage method represents in fact a cultural synthesis. As a cultural synthesis,
collage takes us beyond individualism in the arts. Daniel-
Henry Kahnweiler points out, for example, that Gris and
Picasso understood the essentially impersonal nature of collage, for a great number of their collages are unsigned.[27]
Yet such impersonality is only one pole of modern art,
which oscillates, in Rosenberg's words, between the extremes of the selfless eye and brain and omnipotent identity.[28] This tension is very much present in *Paterson*, Williams's collage poem. For although the overwhelming environment of Paterson casts the poet as a selfless eye, the
poet also incorporates the environment into his work and
thereby radically redefines his art. In this process the poet
becomes so omnipotent that, in effect, whatever he says is

art *is* art, and Williams would agree with Allen Ginsberg's "Beauty is where I hang my hat. And reality. And America" (p. 213). Indeed, the poet is so omnipotent *and* impersonal that his name and the name of his city are the same. Louis Martz notes that *Paterson*—incorporating as it does history, newspapers, conversations, overheard speech, and so on—is in a sense written by the entire milling population of Paterson.[29] The real significance of the method of *Paterson*, however, is that it represents a *cultural collaboration*. Williams's art is a kind of socialist art, for in *Paterson* the culture is creating itself in conversation with the poet, who is barely a poet: "I have defeated myself purposely in almost everything I do because I don't want to be thought an artist. I much prefer to be an ordinary person. I never wanted to be separated from my fellow mortals by acting like an artist. . . . I wanted to be something rare but not to have it separate me from the crowd."[30] Thus in *Paterson* the verbal environment of common usage and the poet enter into a dialectical relationship, in which each continuously transforms the other and neither is allowed to establish a tyranny over the other.

Finally, since Williams is indeed more interested in the "bloody loam" than in the "finished product" (p. 37), *Paterson* represents a thorough vulgarization of structure, and change does in fact show through it. The vulgarization of structure involves rejecting preconceived, formal, and "structuring" structures in favor of more "historical" structures that might have a better chance of capturing

> The vague accuracies of events dancing two
> and two with language which they
> forever surpass . . . (P. 23)

This development in effect equates writing with action, for what becomes important for the writer is not the question of form but the discovery of a kind of writing that has a direct relationship with one's perceptions and that will attest to the authenticity of one's experience. It follows, then, that

The writing is nothing, the being
in a position to write (that's

where they get you) is nine tenths
of the difficulty . . .

.   .   .   .

. . . So that

to write, nine tenths of the problem
is to live. . . . (P. 113)

Thus there must be a life to authenticate the writing, just
as in the long run there must be the writing to authenticate the life. And if Henry James, for example, would emphasize the second half of this equation, Williams would
stress the first. This kind of art would necessitate a certain
vulgarization of structure; more autobiographical, it would
be informed by orders found, not imposed.

Autobiographical writing in general is open-ended and
potentially very congenial to novelty in form, structure, and
language, because it is responsive to the historical particularity of the writer's experience. The historical emphasis
of autobiographical writing, which in effect equates living
and writing, constitutes a continuous source of novelty.
The same historical emphasis underlies avant-garde art in
general, and in avant-garde writing the definition of art
continuously expands, because it is the writer's *attitude* toward his or her material—any material, however unartistic
—that determines whether one's activity is art. As a result,
the danger of the extreme avant-garde position is that its
historical emphasis on the value of change can itself be
undermined: if *anything* is art, it would follow that art is
nothing in particular, and this position does not allow room
for change. Yet the important question for all art is whether it changes. As Alain Jouffroy puts it, "So when does
communication imply something else than its terms alone;
when does it cause us to switch to the other side of what it
has us see and hear? When does it begin to change us by
what it brings us? Is it not at the very moment a change
is made in its own terms? Is not the form of communica-

tion called 'art' that which changes us while changing itself? Hence could 'art' be, by virtue of this fact, the communication of a desire for change? But if so, why this word
art, mummified by the wrappings of respect?"[31]

It is Williams's insistence on and faith in change as a
social and aesthetic value that saves him from a suicidal
avant-gardism, which negates change itself. He writes:
"There is nothing sacred about literature, it is damned from
one end to the other. There is nothing in literature but
change and change is mockery. I'll write whatever I damn
please, whenever I damn please and as I damn please and
it'll be good if the authentic spirit of change is on it" (*SE*,
p. 10). Although he would dissociate art from the Museum
or Library and would have it become inclusive and pro-
fane, he would not say that anything is art, because he affirms change as value. As a result, a curious, homemade
formalism sneaks in through the back door in the form
of his lifelong insistence on "measure" and the "variable
foot," which nevertheless remain more or less mystical.
The social emphasis of his poetry also kept him from losing
sight of the social relationships and interactions that constitute art. Even avant-garde art is based on such communication. For if art is what the artist says is art, and if an
artist is someone who the public says is an artist, art comes
to be partly a matter of belief or faith, since the audience
has to believe in the artist. As we can see from the pas-
sionate acclamations or denunciations that it inspires,
avant-garde art in fact absorbs the energies of both religion and politics. If art is a matter of faith, the object created, chosen, or found by the artist becomes a medium of
communication between the audience and the artist, because they understand each other when they agree to call
X art. And in this act the artist and the audience or society
meet, thereby defining their present, shaping their culture,
and making history. This idea of art as communication between two people that changes both is one way of understanding the concept of change-as-structure. Ultimately,
then, Williams judged the success of a work of art by
whether it communicated. He says of a Cummings poem,

for example, that it is not art for him, because he can "get
no meaning at all" from it (p. 224). And of his own work
he writes:

> . . . what good is it to me
> if you can't understand it?
>   But you got to try hard—[32]

When art is understood as social communication, it
gains seriousness, for in becoming a historical event it assumes moral significance. In return, however, art loses the
privilege of being protected from time; self-consciously historical, it projects its own destruction, since it must necessarily be surpassed. Poe was one of the first literary theorists who not only understood a work of literature as a temporal construct but accepted the full implications of this
view. As a temporal construct, a work dissipates its energy
both within the limits of its first and last lines and in the
course of its public history as a cultural product.[33] Because it is a long poem and because Williams chooses an
explicitly historical structure for his poem, dissipation of
energy characterizes the movement of *Paterson*. Williams
starts out confessing that he does not know where the poem
will lead:

> There is no direction. Whither? I
> cannot say. I cannot say
> more than how. The how (the howl) only
> is at my disposal (proposal) . . . (P. 18)

By Book 4, however, it becomes clear that the progression
of the poem has been more a dissipation: "What I miss,
said your mother, is the poetry, the pure poem of the first
parts" (p. 171), and he asks himself, "Haven't you forgot
your virgin purpose, / the language?" (p. 187).

Williams comes to the defense of his historical, autobiographical form and cites a number of personal, cultural,
and scientific examples of progress through dissipation,
which is simply another instance of creation through destruction. The father-son conflict in this section is one example. The sons—including poetic "sons" like Allen Gins-

berg—will come to replace the fathers: "The best thing a man can do for his son, when he is born, is to die" (p. 171). The splitting of the atom to release energy from matter, embryonic fission leading to birth, the breaking up of the poetic foot to energize the "field" of the page, and the splintering of the epic narrator's voice for the dramatic energy of interacting voices are all processes analogous to the growth of the poem through the dissipation of energy. All are forms of creative destruction, and their use in *Paterson* reflects personal motives. For by Book 4 it is plain that the poem and the poet both evolve through dissipation of energy. The poem *does* leave behind the "pure" poetry of the earlier parts, Williams *is* aging between Book 1 and Book 4, and the world *is* destroying itself in the Korean War. Thus the method of composition-as-decomposition in the long, autobiographical poem not only parallels the progress of the poet, who "composes" and decomposes, but proves adequate to Williams's relationship to his subject-environment:

> ... —in your
> composition and decomposition
> I find my
> despair! (P. 75)

Williams's need to believe that something good will eventually come out of all the destruction is expressed in his formula that dissonance is discovery:

> Dissonance
> (if you are interested)
> leads to discovery (P. 176)

This idea finds support both in the history of science, since

> A dissonance
> in the valence of Uranium
> led to the discovery [of radium,] (P. 176)

and in the image of love as "antagonistic cooperation" that leads to creation. We can read this formula as his justification not only of his subject—Paterson as an environment of dissonance—but of his composite poetic, personal, and public voice and of his literary method of working through the dissonance of poetry and prose in the earlier books. The power and the credibility of his assertion, however, are that it emerges out of his current experience of the drift of *Paterson*, of himself as aging, and of the Korean War. In reading *Paterson*, then, we should keep in mind that Williams took more than ten years to write it. For his form evolved just as his personality evolved—in time. Strictly autobiographical writing simulates the temporal evolution of personality by structuring it as a story. But in *Paterson* personality and form evolve simultaneously, since the recording coincides in time with the experience that it partially creates; indeed, the two are not easily separable:

> nothing is so unclear, between man and
> his writing, as to which is the man and
> which the thing and of them both which
> is the more to be valued (P. 116)

Thus *Paterson* is Williams's autobiography both because it includes a wide variety of facts and details of his daily life and because its growth through destruction represents a formal repetition of the poet's own progress as well as of his current concerns. The poem, like the life it would incorporate, is a temporal structure: its very nature is temporal change. As a result, the poem also embodies the destruction that all creation entails. For it is the ongoing "dissipation" of the poet and the poem that enables both to move on. *Paterson*, then, is so steeped in Williams's life— in his psychic, political, and scientific environment—that its structure is itself part of that environment. The poetic "escape" of *Paterson* lies through—not outside—the nonpoetic experience, for Williams takes his own advice:

> Escape from it—but not by running
> away. Not by "composition." Embrace the
> foulness (P. 103)

Moreover, *as* history *Paterson* itself can only "progress" through literary and cultural history by dissipating its energy. Marcel Duchamp remarks about painting that "after forty or fifty years a picture dies, because its freshness disappears."[34] A painting dies when it no longer inspires painters and new paintings and becomes an object. Williams also believes that the forms of art evolve in conjunction with historical change: "Of course I'm iconoclastic. . . . An artist has to be. A continual break down and build up has to go on. Take the forms in which poems are cast. Most of them are old, not suited to our times. We have to cast about searching for new ones. . . . Pretty soon, they will become old hat. Somebody else will have to work to get rid of them."[35] A poem, then, is a high-energy structure that runs down in time, and the creation of new art involves the destruction of the stabilized old art. Jouffroy describes this kind of destruction as the change of a "permanent order" into a "provisional disorder."[36] "Provisional disorder" suggests that art prepares its history and steps into it; when the provisional disorder reverts back to an order, the work stabilizes and becomes inert, like a piece of lead.

Paterson embodies such a provisional disorder, for it exists as a dialog between order and disorder. As we have seen, its structure is not really a structure; its growth is in fact a dissipation; its "poetry" is always threatening to disintegrate into prose or worse, as in the "poem" on page 137 in which the straight lines of print are violated; and its measure has no measure. "The foot not being fixed," Williams writes, "is only to be described as variable. If the foot itself is variable it allows order in so-called free verse. Thus the verse becomes not free at all but just simply variable, as all things in life properly are."[37] This telling definition of that anomaly the "variable foot" is one more expression of the dialog between art and life that sustains Williams's poetry. Since his forms derive from life and, properly speaking, are not forms at all, the charge of his work is far from dead, as his wide and steady influence attests.

Paterson is a radical poem, because change—social *and*

artistic—is both the ultimate value that the poem upholds
and the supreme reality that it embodies. Williams understood his poem as an act aimed at changing social life and
his art at the same time. The reader's confrontation with
Paterson becomes a kind of action as well, for the poem
requires not merely an intellectual response but a change
of consciousness on the reader's part if it is to become a
"poem." And in forcing the reader to follow the author's
act of self-creation through art, *Paterson* tests the limits of
autobiographical writing: the poet generates his continuous self-creation in a language and form of change, which
in turn lead the reader to reenact the experience of the
work. As history becomes form, then, form itself becomes
a historical experience, a provisional disorder, which transforms both reader and poet. And as the occasion for the
reader's as well as the poet's self-creation, this kind of autobiographical art implies the creation of a new culture, for
it in effect regenerates everyday life.

Frank O'Hara and the Poetics of Love

Frank O'Hara's poetry belongs in an American tradition of
personal poetry that extends back through William Carlos
Williams to Walt Whitman. Although each of these poets
"sings" himself, their self-celebrations are not private or
exclusive; rather, their personal writing is a way of opening "intercourse with the world." And their poetry has immediacy, for not only is it about real people living in historically concrete environments, whether Paterson or Manhattan, but it represents a rediscovery of the language of
speech, which incorporates the "minutia of daily usages"
and depends on the ear alone for its rhythm and measure.
Williams's idea of a "vulgarity of beauty" that surpasses
perfection characterizes this kind of "impure" poetry, in
which the poet is interested more in the processes of perception and self-creation through language than in "poetry"

—more in daily history than in "purity." For example, here is O'Hara's answer to "THE UBIQUITOUS MALLARMÉ": "Is it true you said poems are made of words? / that's only one kind of poem that's true of."[38] Since poems are in fact made of words, however, we cannot take O'Hara literally any more than we can take Whitman at his word when he claims, "the words of my book nothing, the drift of it everything." For Whitman also called *Leaves of Grass* "only a language experiment," and O'Hara admits:

> . . . that
> is all you know words not their feelings
> or what they mean and you write because
> you know them not because you understand them
> ("As Planned," *CP*, p. 382)

When O'Hara "answers" Mallarmé, then, he is making a distinction simply between his kind of "impure" poem and the poem understood as technology—the technology of poem making. For O'Hara, no less than for Whitman, his "great predecessor," words are part of the total complex of experience; more than the raw materials of an art, they are *dramatically* involved in the experience that calls them forth or that they conjure up.

More than words, poems are closer to gestures or acts; whether self-consciously or not, they make history:

> Poetry is not instruments
> that work at times
> then walk out on you
> laugh at you old
> get drunk on you young
> poetry's part of your self
>
> like the passion of a nation
> at war it moves quickly
> provoked to defense or aggression
> unreasoning power
> an instinct for self-declaration

like nations its faults are absorbed
in the heat of sides and angles
combatting the void of rounds
a solid of imperfect placement
nations get worse and worse

but not wrongly revealed
in the universal light of tragedy
          ("To Gottfried Benn," *CP*, pp. 309–310)

O'Hara's understanding of poetry as history precludes the
purity and economy of a closed system such as Poe describes in "The Philosophy of Composition." Thus O'Hara,
as well as his predecessors, would appear to be wasteful.
Yet he does believe in a homely kind of economy: "As for
measure and other technical apparatus, that's just common sense: if you're going to buy a pair of pants you want
them to be tight enough so everyone will want to go to bed
with you."[39] The important distinction between "pure" and
"impure" poems is not that one kind is more or less "art"
or more or less concerned with form than the other, but
that each implies a different attitude toward form. For if
we see the poem as gesture or as dramatic form, poetry is
no longer a question of contents and techniques. The poem
as drama is dialectical; neither life nor art, it represents
their creative interaction. In other words, the poem is on
stage, regenerating both life and art—if we are lucky and
if the poet is not, in O'Hara's phrase, "a plague." Ultimately, then, the test of a poem is what it does for its
animate and inanimate environment.

As drama, the poem is partly a performance by the poet.
The occasional nature of a good many of O'Hara's poems,
as well as his virtuosity or his composing poems on the
spot, suggests that for him writing poetry was something
of a performance. Moreover, just as the definition of "occasion" may expand to include any *particular* incident or
moment, "performance" may come to mean simply the
poet's life—both everyday life and the fast, fast-talking

responses it demands. Everyday life in fact becomes more and more the inspiration of the poems, until O'Hara perfects what he calls his "I do this, I do that" kind of poem, which goes on about what he sees, eats, and drinks and whom he loves, talks to, and so on. For O'Hara agrees with Wallace Stevens that if the quotidian "saps," it also "gives" —like the daily sun—a "humped return." Such poems of the quotidian, when successful, represent a difficult balance between art and life. As Harold Rosenberg remarks about painting, if the work "slips over into action ('life') there is no painting." On the other hand, if form is the artist's exclusive interest and the painting is "satisfied with itself as painting it turns into 'apocalyptic wallpaper.' "[40] In terms of O'Hara's work, the danger is that the poem might slip back into the boredom, the banality, and, ultimately, the defeat of life, for the quotidian also embodies the destructiveness of time. "To Hell with It," which tells the destruction time leaves in its wake, acknowledges the constant struggle between formless life and lifeless form:

> For sentiment is always intruding on form,
>   the immaculate disgust of the mind
> beaten down by pain and the vileness of life's flickering
>   disapproval,
>
>   endless torment pretending to be the rose
> of acknowledgement (courage)
>   and fruitless absolution (hence the word: "hip")
> to be cool,
>   decisive,
>   precise,
>   yes, while the barn door hits you in the face
> each time you get up
>   because the wind, seeing you slim and gallant, rises
>
>   to embrace its darling poet. . . . (CP, p. 276)

Life must be created in art in order to be mastered, but the poem can give only "fruitless absolution" or the false attitude of being able to live with pain—"hence the word:

'hip.' " Thus the writing is both true and false; it is both necessary and falsifying. Indeed, it is just this balance that the writing must strike, for the "immaculate" mind must not overrule the "filthy page of poetry" any more than "sentiment" should take over from "form." Or as O'Hara warns in "Biotherm," the poem must be guarded from *both* "mess and measure."

If such a difficult balance between art and life is to be achieved, however, not only art but everyday life must be redefined or transformed. If the immaculate mind is not to falsify life as "measure," the only way to avoid the "mess" is to avoid boredom and banality in life itself. In his remarks on Larry Rivers and David Smith, O'Hara describes this complete circle of regeneration. He characterizes Rivers's work as a way "to beat the bugaboos of banality and boredom, deliberately invited into the painting and then triumphed over."[41] Just as Rivers brings everyday life into his art, Smith's sculptures bring art into everyday life: "They present a total attention and they are telling you that *that* is the way to be. On guard. In a sense they are benign, because they offer themselves for your pleasure. But beneath that kindness is a warning: don't be bored, don't be lazy, don't be trivial and don't be proud. The slightest loss of attention leads to death."[42] Thus art—and poetry—can transform life, and life continuously changes art, which becomes art precisely by the adequacy of its response to the changingness of life. Consequently, content, technique, and form are secondary to a certain attitude of being wide-awake and open, which alone can triumph over the banal—in art as well as in life. Assuming this attitude, an ordinary life can take on clarity and brilliance, and sudden clarifications of the mess of data and perceptions make for poems. For example, one goes to work every day, but suddenly a day will become "clear"; the "Poem" that begins with "Khrushchev is coming on the right day!" is a good example of this process. Since an attitude of total participation makes for a day just as it makes for a poem, however, the day probably clarifies *because* he is writing a poem about it, for writing a poem is one way of participating in the day: "It may be that poetry makes life's nebulous events tangible to me and restores their detail; or conversely, that poetry brings forth the intangible quality of incidents which are all too concrete and circumstantial. Or each on specific occasions, or both all the time."[43]

This daily urgency to live or to write—whichever we choose to call it—energizes even the least significant of O'Hara's poems. For what saves O'Hara and makes it hard for his imitators is that he is going "on his nerve": "I don't believe in god, so I don't have to make elaborately sounded structures. I hate Vachel Lindsay, always have; I don't even like rhythm, assonance, all that stuff. You just go on your nerve. If someone's chasing you down the street with a knife you just run, you don't turn around and shout, 'Give it up! I was a track star for Mineola Prep.' "[44] This rather drastic identification of experience and art is also the source of the immediacy and speed of O'Hara's poetry:

> I better hurry up and finish this
> before your 3rd goes off the radio
> or I won't know what I'm feeling
> > ("On Rachmaninoff's Birthday #158,"
> > CP, p. 418)

For things are happening, being perceived and recorded all at once because the poet is anything *but* tranquil, what

> . . . with the stream of events
> going so fast and the movingly
> > alternating with the amusingly
> > ("Post the Lake Poets Ballad," CP, p. 336)

Kenneth Koch observes that with O'Hara "it was always an emergency because one's life had to be experienced and reflected on at the same time, and that is just about impossible. He does it in his poems."[45] If both experience and reflection are conceived as total participation in the world, however, the poet can experience life and reflect on it in the same act of *being there* physically, emotionally, intellectually. For even events, O'Hara writes, do not happen without one's "participation."[46] This attitude of total attention characterizes, for example, Jackson Pollock's art, which was truly Action Painting. In his essay on Pollock, O'Hara writes that a "state of spiritual clarity" is "the ultimate goal of the artist": "In this state all becomes clear, and Pollock declared the meanings he had found with astonishing fluency, generosity and expansiveness." The artist, having made a "maximum of decisions" on his ascent to this state of clarity, finally reaches "a limitless space of air and light in which the spirit can act freely and with unpremeditated knowledge. His action is immediately art, not through will, not through esthetic posture, but through a singleness of purpose. . . . Only the artist who has reached this state should be indicated by Harold Rosenberg's well-known designation Action Painter, for only when he is in this state is the artist's 'action' significant purely and simply of itself."[47] This statement would apply to O'Hara as well, for what charges his poems is neither "will" nor "esthetic posture" but an attitude or, in his terms, a "state" of the man himself, which is prior to and contains the form.

Since form emerges from such a state of clarity, the work has unity, regardless of what it contains. Daniel-Henry Kahnweiler writes of the Cubist poets Apollinaire, Reverdy, and Max Jacob that, like the painters, they had "an absolute respect for the unity of the work itself." This unity, which is antirational, derives from "the unity of the feeling from which the work springs. . . . And the Cubist poets, like the painters, conceive of this unity as something absolute, unshakeable and capable of absorbing any kind of heterogeneous element."[48] This description of the Cubists' method echoes O'Hara's account of the method of Action Painting; in both cases the structure of a work is determined not by the demands of preexisting forms but by the shape of the artist's feeling or "state of spiritual clarity" at the time. O'Hara's "Biotherm" is a grand example of this kind of poem, in which the unity of feeling and the attitude of total attention hold the poem together, despite the great variety of things thrown at us with great speed.

This kind of poem always contains the reason for, or the state of, its creation; it cannot become trivial because, when successful, it embodies the pressure that created it. And O'Hara writes under pressure: he does not set out to create immaculate formal constructs. Instead, the shape of a poem—the gesture that it represents as well as its coherence—is determined by need, and the poem records the mind under the pressure of fact, emotion, or life itself at a given moment. Thus O'Hara ends "To Hell with It":

> Wind, you'll have a terrible time
> smothering my clarity, a void
> behind my eyes,
> into which existence
> continues to stuff its wounded limbs
>
> as I make room for them on one
> after another filthy page of poetry.
>
> And mean it. (CP, pp. 276–277)

Accordingly, making statements that are clear or useful to some general, abstract audience cannot be a part of O'Hara's project. A poem is, in Stevens's phrase, "the cry of its occasion"; as such, it may or may not directly "communicate."

If O'Hara is not primarily interested in communicating with a generalized reader, however, he remains very much interested in "grandeur"—in being "poetic." He can say the most "poetic" things in the most "classic" lines, for the everydayness of the facts no more rules out a "poetic" line or perception than poetry repudiates daily life. In the early poem "Today," O'Hara writes with the abandon of the early Stevens:

> Oh! kangaroos, sequins, chocolate sodas!
> You really are beautiful! Pearls,

harmonicas, jujubes, aspirins! all
the stuff they've always talked about

still makes a poem a surprise!
These things are with us every day
even on beachheads and biers. They
do have meaning. They're strong as rocks. (*CP*, p. 15)

The quotidian has meaning because it is the "rock"—it is
the real, which gives even as it takes. Similarly, just as
O'Hara can be everyday *and* "poetic," he can be steeped in
history and at the same time think of posterity as "grandly"
as Keats did. John Ashbery writes that O'Hara was careless
with his poems, half-forgetting them once they were written, because "his thoughts were elsewhere, in the urban
world of fantasy where the poems came from."[49] And yet
O'Hara admonishes his hypothetical assassin-critic:

> . . . Do not

frighten me more than you
have to! I must live forever. ("The Critic," *CP*, p. 48)

Thus he can be poetic and interested in fame because poets
are concerned with such things. In O'Hara's work, "Poetry"
and "the poet" are demythicized and demystified but not
devalued, for he does not relinquish any claims for either.

"In Memory of My Feelings," one of O'Hara's major
poems, was written on his thirtieth birthday and is concerned with the relationship between poetry and life. In
this poem we discover the sources of the kind of thinking
that resulted in increasingly historical and personal poems
after 1956 and that is fully articulated in his "Personism:
A Manifesto" of 1959. Kenneth Koch remarks that "Frank
O'Hara had an ability to fantasize himself to be almost
anybody, anything, anytime, anywhere."[50] "In Memory of
My Feelings" partly charts the progress of such a fluid
consciousness, which, if self-destructive, is still in some
way the source of poetry. The poem opens:

> My quietness has a man in it, he is transparent
> and he carries me quietly, like a gondola, through the
> streets.
> He has several likenesses, like stars and years, like
> numerals.
>
> My quietness has a number of naked selves,
> so many pistols I have borrowed to protect myselves
> from creatures who too readily recognize my weapons
> and have murder in their heart! (CP, pp. 252–253)

The self-destructiveness that is implied here is made explicit with the introduction of the serpent and images of hunting:

> I am underneath its leaves as the hunter crackles and
> pants
> and bursts, as the barrage balloon drifts behind a cloud
> and animal death whips out its flashlight,
>   whistling
> and slipping the glove off the trigger hand. . . .

Thus the serpent—already identified with the "I"—becomes both the hunted and the hunter, and the pistols to protect "myselves" merge with the trigger of the hunter, who seeks to destroy the serpent. This self-destructiveness comes to a head in the image of the vipers, which turn against themselves:

> My transparent selves
> flail about like vipers in a pail, writhing and hissing
> without panic, with a certain justice of response
> and presently the aquiline serpent comes to resemble
> the Medusa.

Yet the serpent is likened to the Medusa, who was the mother of Pegasus, the traditional symbol for poetry. The serpent, then, seems to be specifically the creative self of the poet, as distinct from the transparent man and his likenesses; indeed, the serpent is a suitable symbol for the poet, because it is itself a disguise.

The identity of the hunted and the hunter is a constant theme throughout the poem and shapes O'Hara's vision of his family, the war, and his own past, for the past is also a destroyer:

The dead hunting
and the alive, ahunted.

Among the dead are

My 10   my 19,
my 9,   and the several years. . . .

The sequence of his likenesses—like "years, like numerals"—represents ultimately the progress of death within the poet's consciousness and brings him to the central question of the poem:

rockets splay over a *sposalizio*,
                              fleeing into night
from their Chinese memories, and it is a celebration,
the trying desperately to count them as they die.
But who will stay to be these numbers
when all the lights are dead?

This need for some kind of permanence is restated in the contrast between the anonymous Arabs, who chose life and

. . . didn't stay to count
their inventions, racing into sands, converting them-
    selves into
so many,

and the Greeks, who chose art and left "the pain / at home to be converted into statuary." O'Hara indicates that he preferred the Arabs and asserts:

Grace
to be born and live as variously as possible. . . .

The list of "sordid identifications" that follows, however, maps out a total obliteration of identity and thereby reveals perhaps a loathing of being so utterly in and of time.

Thus the poet's dilemma is clear. On the one hand, he must transform his past into art so that it can no longer hunt him. On the other hand, he must try, as a person, to preserve his past *as history* in order to salvage a continuous and coherent self out of the flow of isolated moments of consciousness—the series of transparent selves. The last lines of the poem focus on this dilemma:

> And yet
> I have forgotten my loves, and chiefly that one, the cancerous
> statue which my body could no longer contain,
> against my will
> against my love
> become art,
> I could not change it into history
> and so remember it,
> and I have lost what is always and everywhere
> present, the scene of my selves, the occasion of these ruses,
> which I myself and singly must now kill
> and save the serpent in their midst.

Art, then, is another form of self-destruction. If, in its recording as art, life becomes conscious, it also becomes permanently fixed. In other words, the past is cancerous and must be exorcised, but the exorcised past no longer belongs to the poet. The danger is that the historical reality of the poet's life and death—"the occasion of these ruses" —is lost in art. At the end of "In Memory of My Feelings," then, O'Hara must shed "these ruses" and save his live, if self-destructive, center in order to go on writing poems that will stay to be all the "numbers / when all the lights are dead." O'Hara presents change as an inner drama of violence, in which one must maintain a balance between one's life and one's art. The poem-recording must be abandoned in the nick of time before it usurps ongoing life, and the poet must surface into the present, change, and history.

Art creates its own geography and constantly threatens to take over life, for the poet's feelings die as words usurp their life, and poems can be written only in memory of feelings. This process is explicit in "Why I Am Not a Painter":

> . . . One day I am thinking of
> a color: orange. I write a line
> about orange. Pretty soon it is a
> whole page of words, not lines.
> Then another page. There should be
> so much more, not of orange, of
> words, of how terrible orange is
> and life. Days go by. It is even in
> prose, I am a real poet. My poem
> is finished and I haven't mentioned
> orange yet. It's twelve poems, I call
> it ORANGES. . . . (CP, p. 262)

O'Hara might have called it "In Memory of Orange."

"In Memory of My Feelings" marks a significant point in O'Hara's career. With this restatement of the essentially Romantic complaint about the falsifications of art, he seems to have transcended the Romantic dichotomy of Art and Life, for he moves on to an understanding of poetry as drama. For example, "In Favor of One's Time," which is another poem about poetry, suggests that the *conflict* of art and life makes for poetry just as it makes for life. In this poem also, we read that the past or the "spent purpose of a perfectly marvellous / life" is the source of poetry. This past or residue, which O'Hara associates with charcoal, "suddenly glimmers and leaps into flame"—much like Shelley's "fading coal, which some invisible influence, like an inconstant wind, awakens to transitory brightness." In O'Hara's terms, too, it is "the quick oxygen in the air" that fans the "blaze," and "however exaggerated at least something's going on." Moreover, O'Hara describes this "blaze of pure sensibility" in "the mirrored room of this consciousness" in words that, oddly enough, recall Stevens, for Stevens also conceives of the imagination as an "incandescence of the intelligence" and calls the poet

> The central man, the human globe, responsive
> As a mirror with a voice, the man of glass,
> Who in a million diamonds sums us up.[51]

In the second stanza, O'Hara is concerned precisely with the struggle between imagination and reality—the self and what is outside it:

> an angel flying slowly, curiously singes its wings
> and you diminish for a moment out of respect
> for beauty then flare up after all that's the angel
> that wrestled with Jacob and loves conflict (*CP*, p. 342)

Since Jacob saw God, "the angel that wrestled with Jacob" is the ultimate reality; since it is also a vision, however, the angel is, at the time time, the ultimate expression of imagination. This fusion of imagination and reality also characterizes Stevens's conception of the "necessary angel of earth" in whose sight we "see the earth again," and Stevens's angel, like O'Hara's, can exist only as a conflict of two equal forces. In O'Hara's words:

> . . . we're off into
> an immortal contest of actuality and pride
> which is love assuming the consciousness of itself
> as sky over all, medium of finding and founding
> not just resemblance but the magnetic otherness
> that that that stands erect in the spirit's glare
> and waits for the joining of an opposite force's breath.

From the conflict of "actuality and pride" or reality and imagination, love emerges conscious of itself as "sky over all," and love—the conflict/fusion of these two forces—discovers and establishes not only "resemblance" but the "magnetic otherness" of the self and the world. Thus poetry, which O'Hara equates here with love, preserves the

"magnetic otherness" of the self and the world; the use of
"erect" gives sexual overtones to this union-in-conflict.

"Personism: A Manifesto," which was written at about
the same time as this poem, fully articulates O'Hara's
"poetics" of love. In this manifesto-as-mock-manifesto,
O'Hara announces that Personism "puts the poem squarely
between the poet and the person. . . . The poem is at last
between two persons instead of two pages." More specifically, "one of its minimal aspects is to address itself to one
person (other than the poet himself), thus evoking overtones of love without destroying love's life-giving vulgarity,
and sustaining the poet's feelings towards the poem while
preventing love from distracting him into feeling about the
person." And the details of O'Hara's founding this "movement" are telling: "It was founded by me after lunch with
LeRoi Jones on August 27, 1959, a day in which I was in
love with someone (not Roi, by the way, a blond). I went
back to work and wrote a poem for this person. While I
was writing it I was realizing that if I wanted to I could
use the telephone instead of writing the poem, and so Personism was born" (*CP*, p. 499). This manifesto defends
the kind of dramatic poetry that always interested O'Hara,
for a good number of his poems are addressed to particular
people, either explicitly or implicitly:

> When anyone reads this but you it begins
> to be lost. My voice is sucked into a thousand
> ears and I don't know whether I'm weakened.
> ("A Letter to Bunny," *CP*, p. 23)

Addressing particular readers is one way of retaining dramatic particularity or a sense of the real-life, dramatic
encounter that called forth the poem; another way is to attach personal and particular significance to facts. In
"Christmas Card to Grace Hartigan," for example, O'Hara
writes:

> For red there is our blood

> which, like your smile, must be
> protected from spilling into
> generality by secret meanings, (CP, p. 212)

In this way poems can be loaded with "feeling" yet remain taut, specific, and credible.

Moreover, Personism offers a solution to the problem of "In Memory of My Feelings." In Personism we see how the poet's history—his present love—may be changed into art without being falsified. Inspired by love for a particular person, the poem becomes itself the object of love, which the poet loves precisely because it is inspired by love. Thus the poem retains the historical immediacy and the "marvellousness" of life, the "overtones of love," and "love's life-giving vulgarity" and still remains a poem, for love—in being transferred to the poem—sustains "the poet's feelings towards the poem while preventing love from distracting him into feeling about the person." In Personism, then, history is converted into drama, and poetry becomes a communication with, and a participation in, actuality. Experience is significant only insofar as it is the particular experience of a particular person. In his poetry of love, O'Hara not only retains the historical particularity of his experience but achieves the ideal of true and total participation in the world, which means "to move is to love." For love is communication with the total environment, especially since—O'Hara would agree with Whitman—"a kelson of the creation is love." In O'Hara's words, "And if love lives at all in the cheap tempestuousness of our time, I think it can only be in the unrelenting honesty with which we face animate nature and inanimate things and the cruelty of our kind, and perceive and articulate and, like Zhivago, choose love above all else" (CP, p. 509). Moreover, love and poetry are both ways of achieving immortality, which had been one of the main concerns of "In Memory of My Feelings": "You in others—this is your soul. This is what you are," O'Hara quotes Zhivago, "your soul, your immortality, your life in others" (CP, p. 504). Thus

O'Hara's tone in "Personism" should not mislead us; if he can be "killingly funny," he can also be deadly serious. For Personism and the poetics of love *work*: they answer poetic and personal needs at once.

Given this way of looking at O'Hara's career, it is beside the point to insist that we must look at the *Collected Poems* as poems and that O'Hara's personality and life are irrelevant. This same attitude is behind the criticism that the *Collected Poems* needed a good editor to weed things out. As Kenneth Koch says, the *Collected Poems* offers us not one great poem but "a collection of created moments that illuminate a whole life."[52] And the "whole life," in turn, illuminates the poems, separately and all together. We cannot isolate O'Hara's work from his life and the pressures of his environment without running the risk of being irrelevant ourselves. O'Hara puts himself on the line in a special way, since his poetics of love implicates even his readers. The poem as drama is a multilayered construct, to which we may apply Kenneth Burke's distinction between play audience and theater audience.[53] While O'Hara maintains the particularity of his play audience, or the person whom the poem addresses, he in effect also maintains the dramatic particularity of his readers, or his theater audience. Thus the reader is not generalized either; he or she remains a particular person, listening and sometimes eavesdropping. In this kind of relationship, O'Hara's personality becomes rather important. We do not have to love Stevens in order to read and like his work, but we do in a sense have at least to like O'Hara in order to enjoy his poems, just as we have to like Whitman in order to enjoy *his* poetry. According to Freud, poets write because they want to be loved—by everyone. Whitman and O'Hara make no secret of this, and we must respond, because we are in their confidence. In their kind of autobiographical writing, there is an indeterminacy principle at work, and the relationship between the poet's personality and his work is *in principle* incalculable. If we focus on the poems alone, the man or the force that makes them poems is obscured, so that the question arises whether a number of them are even poems; on the other hand, if we focus on the personality exclusively, the poetry becomes a blur. We can glorify the personality or the poetry alone, but either way we miss the pure *and* confused wholeness of the man's experience and his art together opening "intercourse with the world":

> And the purity
> of my confusion is
> there, it's poetry
>
> in love with you
> along with me,
> both of us love you
> in the same "My!" ("A Hill," CP, pp. 203–204)

Coda
New Life in a New World

*In our inability to live the life of a creator can be found
the meaning of the fall of man. . . . What is the* raison
d'être, *what is the explanation of the seemingly insane
drive of man to be painter and poet if it is not an act of
defiance against man's fall and an assertion that he return
to the Adam of the Garden of Eden? For the artists are
the first men.*

—BARNETT NEWMAN

American writers have found autobiographical or personal
literature particularly congenial, for such writing affirms
the power of individuals to create not only themselves as
heroes but a social environment—a whole culture. From
Henry David Thoreau to Frank O'Hara, we have seen the
American autobiographical writer becoming a heroic figure
in a defiant assertion of the artist's power to shape real
people and a real civilization. This process informs other
American autobiographies as well. The creative power of
autobiography is fully exercised in as early a work as *The
Autobiography of Benjamin Franklin*, which not only creates a Ben Franklin who is representative of the emerging
bourgeois nation but through this character articulates the
values that will in fact shape the emerging nation. In the
hands of Franklin, autobiography was primarily a rhetorical mode, for he was consciously exploiting the power of
the autobiographical hero "I" to shape a world. A later and
somewhat different example of the wholesale creation of an
environment is Gertrude Stein's *The Autobiography of
Alice B. Toklas*. Although in this book Stein is a personage
and a personality presumably seen from the outside, she is
still the creative force of the work, for her personality becomes a compositional center. Here personality—not con-

sciousness or moral character—coincides exactly with the dimensions of the text. By simply re-collecting modern painters and paintings, new writers and musicians, sundry friends and much gossip—by simply seeing all these things in the light of the personality "Gertrude Stein"—she composes a composite "modern experience" with herself as the center. It is not surprising that George Washington is one of her heroes, for as commander of the avant-garde forces Stein is engaged in nothing less than making history and making it American.

Indeed, the autobiographical mode commands so much power that it can become a political weapon. In autobiography the very means of telling one's story—in the first person and from the inside, so to speak—are an assertion of the power of the teller and establish the credibility of one's story. It is for this reason that autobiographical writing has proved so useful to oppressed peoples. For example, autobiography has become the predominant form of black literature in America because it commands the potentially political power to change minds. The career of a writer like Richard Wright demonstrates the usefulness of autobiography. Only in *Black Boy*, where Wright speaks as an autobiographer, does he succeed in transcending the stereotypes of blacks as victims or criminals and come into possession of himself as a black and as an American undergoing the archetypal American journey of self-discovery or self-creation. And when Wright tells his own story, the act of writing becomes necessary, because his need to tell his story is central to his subject of discovering himself as a person and a writer. Simply by speaking in the first person, then, he achieves his goal of necessary and human speech and thereby escapes the vicious circle of a black author addressing the white oppressor-audience through the common medium of black stereotypes.

Another kind of creative power, however, also seems inherent in autobiographical writing; as a recent work of self-advertisement like *A Moveable Feast* demonstrates, repetition itself is creative. However inaccurate in its details, *A Moveable Feast* is a true autobiography, because it affirms the creative power of repetition. Hemingway succeeds in quite literally recapturing his youth, for in this book he is able to write once more with the naturalness and spontaneity of his youthful style before it became the "Hemingway style." Thus what had eluded Hemingway in his later fictional works opened up and became available to him in his autobiography. Just as autobiographical writing as repetition has a kind of conjuring power, as retrospection also it is creative, for memory looks out upon new landscapes. As William Carlos Williams puts it:

The descent beckons
          as the ascent beckoned
                    Memory is a kind
of accomplishment
          a sort of renewal
                    even
an initiation, since the spaces it opens are new
places
          inhabited by hordes
                    heretofore unrealized,
of new kinds—
          since their movements
                    are towards new objectives
(even though formerly they were abandoned)

No defeat is made up entirely of defeat—since
the world it opens is always a place
          formerly
                    unsuspected. A
world lost,
          a world unsuspected
                    beckons to new places
and no whiteness (lost) is so white as the memory
of whiteness   . (*Paterson*, pp. 77–78)

Autobiographical writing also affirms the power of American writers to create literature itself in their own

image. For if autobiographical writing is one way of creating American heroes and defining American culture, it is
also a source of continual stylistic innovation. As such,
personal writing in effect substitutes for a literary tradition
without restricting the writer, for in this kind of writing
the style and the person must be one and inseparable. Thus
one must go it alone anyway and discover one's own style
and forms, and the absence of a tradition is no longer a
problem. Moreover, since style creates not only literature
but a person, it becomes something more than a literary
strategy: style becomes part of the writer's total strategy
for living. As we have seen, in autobiographical works
literary and nonliterary questions and answers, problems
and solutions, are one and the same. Each of the works I
have studied represents a dialog of the artist, the art available to him, his psychic life, his culture, and his times.
Thus creators of such works create at once themselves as
artists and as persons, their culture, and their art, and by
asserting their power as the creators of the totality of their
existence, they resurrect themselves as people before the
Fall.

Notes

INTRODUCTION

1. Georges Poulet writes, "It is characteristic of a work at once to create its structures and to transcend them, I should even say to destroy them. So the work of an author is certainly the collection of texts which he has written, but in the sense that as they follow one another, each replaces the last and reveals thereby a movement toward a liberation from structures." See J. Hillis Miller, "The Geneva School: The Criticism of Marcel Raymond, Albert Béguin, Georges Poulet, Jean Rousset, Jean-Pierre Richard, and Jean Starobinski," in *Modern French Criticism*, ed. John K. Simon, p. 280. If we understand this movement not as a liberation from *structure* but as a liberation from the structures that have already been developed or that have become convention, this progression could serve to characterize the history of literature itself, as well as the career of one writer.

2. Maurice Merleau-Ponty, *Signs*, trans. Richard C. McCleary, pp. 62–63.

3. I am indebted to Kenneth Burke's "Literature as Equipment for Living" (*The Philosophy of Literary Form*, pp. 253–262) for suggesting this term to me.

4. Susanne K. Langer, *Philosophy in a New Key*, pp. 134, 140.

5. D. H. Lawrence to A. W. McLeod, October 26, 1913, in *The Collected Letters of D. H. Lawrence*, ed. Harry T. Moore, 1:234.

6. Sigmund Freud, *Beyond the Pleasure Principle*, ed. and trans. James Strachey. See especially pp. 34–36.

7. Roy Pascal, *Design and Truth in Autobiography*, p. 43.

8. Roland Barthes, *Writing Degree Zero*, trans. Annette Lavers and Colin Smith, p. 39.

9. Freud, *Beyond the Pleasure Principle*, pp. 70–71.

10. Harold Rosenberg, "The Art Object and the Esthetics of Impermanence," in his *The Anxious Object*, p. 89.

11. Henri Focillon, *The Life of Forms in Art*, trans. Charles Beecher Hogan and George Kubler, p. 55. See also pp. 62–63.
12. Alain Robbe-Grillet, *For a New Novel*, trans. Richard Howard, pp. 152–154.
13. Jean Starobinski, "The Style of Autobiography," in *Literary Style*, ed. and trans. Seymour Chatman, p. 289.

THE ECONOMIES OF *Walden*

1. Henry David Thoreau, *Walden*, ed. J. Lyndon Shanley, p. 3. Hereafter the page number will be cited in the text.
2. Among Thoreau's recent critics, Charles R. Anderson, e.g., writes of *Walden* that "the chronicle aspect, as indeed the whole mode of autobiography, is more a device for maneuvering than a strict form. The author himself confesses that he reduced the two years and more of his actual residence to one, 'for convenience.' " See *The Magic Circle of Walden*, p. 39. According to Anderson, autobiography in *Walden* is only the author's mask, and the real theme is the discovery of the self (ibid., p. 17). Thus Anderson seems to use autobiography to refer to factual reportage, which in my view is an impossible abstraction. As we shall see, autobiography is only half history; the other half is fiction, and the kind of autobiography that can be called literature is always concerned precisely with self-discovery.
3. J. Lyndon Shanley's findings indicate that Thoreau must have begun writing the first version sometime in late 1846 or early 1847. See *The Making of* Walden, p. 24.
4. Alfred Kazin, "Autobiography as Narrative," *Michigan Quarterly Review* 3, no. 4 (Fall 1964): 213.
5. Bertil Romberg, *Studies in the Narrative Technique of the First-Person Novel*, trans. Michael Taylor and Harold H. Borland, p. 59.
6. Henry David Thoreau, *The Writings of Henry David Thoreau*, ed. Bradford Torrey, 9 (*Journal* 3):232. In this edition, the volumes of the *Journal* are numbered separately from the volumes of the *Writings*. Hereafter the *Journal* will be cited in the text as *J*, followed by the volume and page numbers.

7. Ovid, *The Metamorphoses*, trans. Horace Gregory, p. 97. Subsequent references to the legend of Echo and Narcissus will be from this version.

8. Ralph Waldo Emerson, "Thoreau," in *The Complete Works of Ralph Waldo Emerson*, ed. Edward Waldo Emerson, 10:481.

9. Herman Melville, *Moby-Dick*, ed. Charles Feidelson, Jr., p. 26.

10. Saint Augustine, *Confessions*, trans. R. S. Pine-Coffin, pp. 222–223.

11. Melville, *Moby-Dick*, p. 215.

12. William Wordsworth to Sir George Beaumont, May 1, 1805, in *The Early Letters of William and Dorothy Wordsworth (1787–1805)*, ed. Ernest de Selincourt, p. 489.

13. Emerson, "Thoreau," p. 454.

14. Georges Poulet, "Phenomenology of Reading," *New Literary History* 1, no. 1 (Fall 1969): 58.

15. James Russell Lowell, "Thoreau," in *The Writings of James Russell Lowell*, 1:371.

16. Herbert Marcuse, *Eros and Civilization*, p. 153.

17. Lowell, "Thoreau," p. 375.

18. See, e.g., Sherman Paul, *The Shores of America*, pp. 256–279.

19. Shanley, *The Making of* Walden, p. 7.

20. Kenneth Burke, *Language as Symbolic Action*, p. 27.

21. Paul, *The Shores of America*, p. 326.

22. Anderson, *The Magic Circle of Walden*, pp. 213–257.

23. Henry David Thoreau, *Consciousness in Concord*, ed. Perry Miller, pp. 126–127.

24. Joseph J. Moldenhauer, "Paradox in *Walden*," in *Twentieth Century Interpretations of Walden*, ed. Richard Ruland, pp. 80–81.

25. Emerson, "Thoreau," p. 470.

26. Ralph Waldo Emerson, in *Henry David Thoreau*, by Joseph Wood Krutch, p. 201.

27. Emerson, "Thoreau," p. 455.

28. Krutch, *Henry David Thoreau*, pp. 200–201.

29. David Skwire, "A Check List of Wordplays in *Walden*," *American Literature* 31, no. 3 (November 1959): 282–289.

30. Sigmund Freud, *Jokes and Their Relation to the Unconscious*, trans. James Strachey, pp. 42, 119.

31. Ibid., pp. 120, 122.
32. Miller, in Thoreau, *Consciousness in Concord*, p. 33.
33. Shanley, *The Making of* Walden, p. 63.
34. Miller, in Thoreau, *Consciousness in Concord*, p. 110.
35. Robert Frost, "Thoreau's *Walden*," *The Listener*, August 26, 1954, p. 319.
36. Paul Zweig, *The Heresy of Self-Love*, p. 257.
37. Ibid., p. 171.
38. Ellery Channing to Thoreau, March 5, 1845, in *The Correspondence of Henry David Thoreau*, ed. Walter Harding and Carl Bode, p. 161.
39. Lowell, "Thoreau," pp. 374–375.
40. Poulet, "Phenomenology of Reading," p. 58.

"WALT WHITMAN, A KOSMOS, OF MANHATTAN THE SON"

1. Walt Whitman, "Song of Myself," in his *Leaves of Grass*, ed. Harold W. Blodgett and Sculley Bradley, sec. 4. Hereafter section numbers will be given in the text.
2. Robert Langbaum, *The Poetry of Experience*, pp. 35, 47.
3. Ernst Cassirer, *Language and Myth*, trans. Susanne K. Langer, pp. 10, 58, 98.
4. Langer, *Philosophy in a New Key*, pp. 156, 157.
5. Ernst Cassirer, *Mythical Thought*, vol. 2 of his *The Philosophy of Symbolic Forms*, trans. Ralph Manheim, p. 109.
6. F. O. Matthiessen, *American Renaissance*, p. 564.
7. Ibid., pp. 530–531; John F. Lynen, *The Design of the Present*, p. 326.
8. Emerson, "The Poet," in *The Complete Works of Ralph Waldo Emerson*, 3:6; Gertrude Stein, *Narration*, p. 34.
9. Roger Asselineau, *The Evolution of Walt Whitman*, trans. Richard P. Adams; R. W. B. Lewis, "Walt Whitman: Always Going Out and Coming In," in his *Trials of the Word*, pp. 3–35.
10. Kenneth Burke, "Policy Made Personal," in *Leaves of Grass: One Hundred Years After*, ed. Milton Hindus, p. 101.
11. Friedrich Nietzsche, *The Birth of Tragedy and the Genealogy of Morals*, trans. Francis Golffing, p. 38.
12. C. G. Jung, *Aion*, trans. R. F. C. Hull, pp. 63, 61.
13. Whitman, *Leaves of Grass*, p. 1.
14. Matthiessen, *American Renaissance*, p. 535; Edwin Havi-

land Miller, *Walt Whitman's Poetry*, pp. 21–22; Quentin Anderson, *The Imperial Self*, pp. 98–101.

15. Randall Jarrell, *Poetry and the Age*, pp. 125–126.

16. Walt Whitman, "Preface, 1876," in *The Collected Prose*, vol. 2 of *The Works of Walt Whitman*, p. 294.

17. Sigmund Freud, "The Antithetical Sense of Primal Words," in his *Character and Culture*, ed. Philip Rieff, pp. 45, 49.

18. D. H. Lawrence, *Studies in Classic American Literature*, pp. 174–176.

19. Arguing for "Song of Myself" as an American epic, Roy Harvey Pearce in effect redefines "epic" in order to apply the term to Whitman's poem. According to Pearce, "the heroism of modern society has infinitely more aspects and qualities than can be fused in the single hero of the traditional epic"; the new epic "cannot be in form like the traditional epic," and "it cannot teach by example, as did the traditional epic." Moreover, "as the traditional epic had achieved its authenticity through confirmation, so the new epic would achieve its authenticity through creation and re-creation." Thus "Song of Myself" becomes an epic that exhibits none of the qualities of an epic. See *The Continuity of American Poetry*, pp. 71, 72.

20. Lynen, *The Design of the Present*, pp. 289–290, 325. This ahistorical view of the poem leads Lynen to make such statements as "while certain clusters of lyrics—27, 28, and 29, for example—obviously fit together, one feels that many others could be rearranged without serious loss" (p. 291).

21. Basil de Selincourt, *Walt Whitman*, pp. 96–97, 98.

22. Gay Wilson Allen, "Biblical Analogies for Walt Whitman's Prosody," *Revue Anglo-Américaine* 10, no. 6 (August 1933): 490–507.

23. De Selincourt, *Walt Whitman*, p. 27; Miller, *Walt Whitman's Poetry*, pp. 4, 6.

24. Asselineau, *The Evolution of Walt Whitman*, p. 16.

25. Gay Wilson Allen, *The Solitary Singer*, pp. 110, 117.

26. Malcolm Cowley, Introduction to *Walt Whitman's Leaves of Grass*, ed. Malcolm Cowley, p. xxxiii.

27. Walt Whitman, "Preface, 1855," in *The Collected Prose*, p. 273.

28. Starobinski, "The Style of Autobiography," p. 291.

29. Walt Whitman, "A Backward Glance O'er Travel'd Roads," in *Leaves of Grass*, p. 563.

30. Cowley, Introduction, p. xiv; John Kinnaird, "*Leaves of Grass* and the American Paradox," in *Whitman*, ed. Roy Harvey Pearce, p. 34.

31. Allen, *The Solitary Singer*, pp. 134–135; Asselineau, *The Evolution of Walt Whitman*, pp. 17–46.

32. Walt Whitman, "American National Literature," in *The Collected Prose*, p. 505.

33. Perry Miller, "The Shaping of the American Character," *New England Quarterly* 28, no. 4 (December 1955): 453.

34. Georg Misch, *A History of Autobiography in Antiquity*, trans. E. W. Dickes, 1:13.

35. Jorge Luis Borges, "Note on Walt Whitman," in *Other Inquisitions*, trans. Ruth L. C. Simms, p. 70.

36. Whitman, *Leaves of Grass*, p. 4.

37. Whitman, "Preface, 1855," p. 279.

38. Walt Whitman, "The Bible as Poetry," in *The Collected Prose*, p. 398.

HENRY JAMES'S PREFACES, OR THE STORY OF THE STORIES

1. See, e.g., R. P. Blackmur's Introduction to the Prefaces in Henry James, *The Art of the Novel*. Leon Edel, in *Henry James*, also views the Prefaces mainly as criticism or, in James's words to William D. Howells, as "a sort of plea for Criticism, for Discrimination, for Appreciation on other than infantile lines" (August 17, 1908, in *The Letters of Henry James*, ed. Percy Lubbock, 2:99). C. F. Burgess, on the other hand, reads the Prefaces for the insights they provide into the creative process. See "The Seeds of Art: Henry James's *Donnée*," *Literature and Psychology* 8, no. 3 (Summer 1963): 67–73. Finally, although René Wellek takes issue with Blackmur's high praise of the Prefaces as criticism and finds them disappointing as criticism, he does not offer an alternative approach beyond noting that the Prefaces have "the almost unique distinction of being an author's extended commentary on his own work." See *The Later Nineteenth Century*, vol. 4 of his *A History of Modern Criticism 1750–1950*, p. 213.

2. James, *The Art of the Novel*, p. 4. Hereafter page numbers will be given in the text.

3. Edgar Allan Poe, "The Philosophy of Composition," in *The*

Complete Works of Edgar Allan Poe, ed. James A. Harrison, 14:193.
4. Paul Valéry, "Memoirs of a Poem," in his The Art of Poetry, trans. Denise Folliot, p. 103.
5. Wolfgang Iser, "The Reading Process: A Phenomenological Approach," New Literary History 3, no. 2 (Winter 1972): 279, 283–284.
6. Roland Barthes, "Action Sequences," in Patterns of Literary Style, ed. Joseph P. Strelka, p. 9.
7. Jean-Paul Sartre, Nausea, trans. Lloyd Alexander, p. 57.
8. Although this passage can be found in ibid., pp. 57–58, here I am using the more lucid translation found in Jean-Paul Sartre, The Philosophy of Jean-Paul Sartre, ed. Robert D. Cumming, p. 59.
9. Valéry, "Memoirs of a Poem," p. 104.
10. Barthes, "Action Sequences," p. 11.
11. Ibid., p. 14.
12. Georges Poulet, Studies in Human Time, trans. Elliott Coleman, p. 353.
13. Ibid., p. 354.
14. Edmund Husserl, The Phenomenology of Internal Time-Consciousness, ed. Martin Heidegger, trans. James S. Churchill, p. 76.
15. Daniel Aaron, "The Treachery of Recollection: The Inner and the Outer History," in Essays on History and Literature, ed. Robert H. Bremner, p. 10.
16. John Paterson, who has noted the images of adventure in James's writings in general, takes such imagery to mean that for James the inner life was as fraught with peril as any adventure of Tom Sawyer. See "The Language of 'Adventure' in Henry James," American Literature 32, no. 3 (November 1960): 291–301. More to our purpose, however, is a story like James's "The Jolly Corner," in which the imagery of danger and adventure is specifically associated with meeting the double, the journey into the past, and self-consciousness in general.
17. Saint Augustine, Confessions, pp. 218–219.
18. Mary McCarthy, "A Guide to Exiles, Expatriates, and Internal Emigrés," New York Review of Books, March 9, 1972, p. 6.
19. Henry James, "The Art of Fiction," in his Partial Portraits, p. 388.

20. Emerson, "The Poet," p. 37.
21. Søren Kierkegaard, *Repetition*, trans. Walter Lowrie, p. 135.
22. Wallace Stevens, *The Collected Poems of Wallace Stevens*, p. 406.
23. R. P. Blackmur, "In the Country of the Blue," *Kenyon Review* 5, no. 4 (Autumn 1943): 598.
24. Anderson, *The Imperial Self*.

HENRY ADAMS, CONNOISSEUR OF CHAOS

1. Henry Adams, *The Education of Henry Adams*, p. 451. Hereafter page numbers will be cited in the text.
2. Kenneth Burke, *Permanence and Change*, pp. 93, 94.
3. See Edward Lurie, "American Scholarship: A Subjective Interpretation of Nineteenth-Century Cultural History," in *Essays on History and Literature*, ed. Bremner, pp. 31–80; Max I. Baym, "Henry Adams and the Critics," *American Scholar* 15, no. 1 (Winter 1945–46): 79–89; Edgar Johnson, "Henry Adams: The Last Liberal," *Science and Society* 1, no. 3 (Spring 1937): 362–377; Yvor Winters, "Henry Adams, or the Creation of Confusion," in his *In Defense of Reason*, p. 405; Robert F. Sayre, *The Examined Self*; and Gerrit H. Roelofs, "Henry Adams: Pessimism and the Intelligent Use of Doom," *ELH* 17, no. 3 (September 1950): 214–239.
4. Burke, *Permanence and Change*, p. 98.
5. According to Max Baym, Hamlet as the prototypical failure-as-hero is the precursor of the nineteenth-century figures like Byron and Shelley who are the immediate models for Adams's hero. This view, however, greatly simplifies Adams, not to mention Hamlet, for to judge Adams's failure as a "pen and paper failure" that it "pleased his artistic fancy" to assume is to project the image of a man who secretly patted himself on the back while posing as a failure. See "Henry Adams and the Critics," pp. 86, 88. When applied to Adams, this image is unpleasant and uninteresting, not because he is *not* posing—for like Hamlet he is always acting—but because he does not know with half the assurance of Baym what part or on which stage he is playing. Indeed, had Adams known his role, he might have been a "success." Charles Vandersee's more thorough study of the

parallels between Hamlet and Adams is much more persuasive. According to Vandersee, "conscience" and "consciousness," which "exist inextricably" in Hamlet's character, inform respectively the first and second major parts of the *Education*. Vandersee maintains that Adams consciously cast himself as an American Hamlet and points out that Adams's other writings reveal extensive familiarity with the play. See his "The Hamlet in Henry Adams," in *Shakespeare Survey*, vol. 24, ed. Kenneth Muir.

6. Henry Adams, "Buddha and Brahma," *Yale Review* 5, no. 1 (October 1915): 85.

7. Henry Adams to Charles Francis Adams, November 21, 1862, in *A Cycle of Adams Letters*, ed. Worthington Chauncey Ford, 1:195.

8. Henry Adams to Henry Osborn Taylor, November 22, 1909, in *Letters of Henry Adams (1892–1918)*, ed. Worthington Chauncey Ford, p. 526. Hereafter referred to as *Letters (1892–1918)*.

9. Lurie, "American Scholarship," pp. 34, 40, 36.

10. Henry Adams, *Democracy*, pp. 24, 42.

11. William H. Jordy, *Henry Adams*, p. 268.

12. From September 6, 1839, in *The Journals of Søren Kierkegaard*, ed. and trans. Alexander Dru, p. 80.

13. Kenneth Burke, *Attitudes toward History*, p. 49.

14. G. Wilson Knight, *The Wheel of Fire*, pp. 31, 32.

15. James Kirsch, *Shakespeare's Royal Self*, pp. 160, 165.

16. Adams to Elizabeth Cameron, December 12, 1891, in *Henry Adams*, by Ernest Samuels, p. 74.

17. J. C. Levenson, *The Mind and Art of Henry Adams*, p. 335.

18. Adams to John Hay, January 23, 1883, in *Letters of Henry Adams (1858–1891)*, ed. Worthington Chauncey Ford, p. 347. Hereafter referred to as *Letters (1858–1891)*.

19. Adams to Henry James, May 6, 1908, in *Letters (1892–1918)*, p. 495.

20. William Willeford, *The Fool and His Scepter*, pp. 157–158, 194–196, 198.

21. Francis Fergusson, *The Idea of a Theater*, p. 115.

22. Willeford, *The Fool and His Scepter*, p. 16.

23. Adams to Brooks Adams, January 30, 1910, in *Letters (1892–1918)*, p. 532.

24. George Hochfield, e.g., claims that the pattern of "quest ending in failure" is the "quintessential drama" of Adams's

mind in *all* his books (*Henry Adams*, p. 130). Carl L.
Becker regards "the light showers of wit and sarcasm" as
"mostly protective coloring," since at bottom Adams failed
even to "unravel the riddle of his own failure"; for this
reason, Becker concludes, "there was an element of tragedy" in Adams's life ("The Education of Henry Adams," in
his *Everyman His Own Historian*, pp. 155–156). R. P.
Blackmur, on the other hand, would make of Adams's failure a human tragedy: "Death is the expense of life and failure is the expense of greatness" ("The Expense of Greatness:
Three Emphases on Henry Adams," in his *The Expense
of Greatness*, p. 274). Max Baym considers Adams a "pen
and paper failure," and Gerrit Roelofs, who begins by dis-
agreeing with Baym, goes on to prove that the theme of
failure is "largely a literary and rhetorical device" (Baym,
"Henry Adams and the Critics," p. 88; Roelofs, "Henry
Adams," pp. 215, 230). Louis Kronenberger alone has seen
why the *Education* falls short of tragedy; in his view, "a
lifetime of self-analysis" does not "compensate for a failure
to see things morally" ("The Education of Henry Adams,"
in *Books That Changed Our Minds*, ed. Malcolm Cowley
and Bernard Smith, p. 56). According to Kronenberger,
then, Adams failed even to become a tragic hero. However,
even a critic like Robert Sayre, who does not share the
standard view of the *Education* as a tragedy, sees Adams
as heroic, for he regards his story as an epic. Yet the epic—
no less than tragedy—is possible only under certain social
conditions. Sayre is aware that the *Education* "is not moved
by the unities of its culture but by the disunities," and he
defends his use of "epic" only by drastically redefining it
(*The Examined Self*, pp. 200, 201).

25. In my discussion of comedy in this chapter, I am indebted
    to Wylie Sypher's "The Meanings of Comedy," in *Comedy*,
    by Henri Bergson and George Meredith, pp. 193–255.
26. See, e.g., Winters, "Henry Adams, or the Creation of Con-
    fusion," p. 398.
27. Sypher, "The Meanings of Comedy," pp. 204–205, 196.
28. Merleau-Ponty, *Signs*, p. 3.
29. Adams to Charles Milnes Gaskell, April 18, 1871, in *Letters
    (1858–1891)*, p. 206.
30. Adams to Elizabeth Cameron, July 22, 1911, in *Letters
    (1892–1918)*, p. 570.

31. Adams to Charles Francis Adams, October 10, 1910, in ibid., p. 551.
32. Sigmund Freud, "On the Mechanism of Paranoia," in his *General Psychological Theory*, ed. Philip Rieff, pp. 39, 40, 42.
33. Charles Vandersee, "The Four Menageries of Henry Adams," *Arizona Quarterly* 24, no. 4 (Winter 1968): 293–308.
34. See, e.g., Douglas C. Muecke, *The Compass of Irony*, p. 31.
35. See ibid., pp. 201–202, 198.
36. Adams to Elizabeth Cameron, January 24, 1910, in *Letters* (*1892–1918*), p. 531.
37. Thomas Carlyle, *Heroes and Hero-Worship*, in *The Collected Works of Thomas Carlyle*, 14:400.
38. Stephen Spender, "Confessions and Autobiography," in his *The Making of a Poem*, p. 64.
39. Sayre, *The Examined Self*, p. 121.
40. Adams to Whitelaw Reid, September 9, 1908, in *Henry Adams and His Friends*, ed. Harold Dean Cater, p. 621.
41. Francis Cornford, *The Origin of Attic Comedy*, pp. 206, 204.
42. Kenneth Burke, "The Virtues and Limitations of Debunking," in his *The Philosophy of Literary Form*, pp. 147–148.
43. Fergusson, *The Idea of a Theater*, p. 129.
44. Sypher, "The Meanings of Comedy," pp. 242, 247.
45. Adams to William James, February 11, 1908, in *Letters* (*1892–1918*), p. 490.
46. Emily Dickinson, *The Poems of Emily Dickinson*, ed. Thomas H. Johnson, 2:434.
47. Stevens, *Collected Poems*, p. 215.

TWO POETS

1. Wylie Sypher, *Rococo to Cubism in Art and Literature*, p. 74.
2. Henri Lefebvre, *Everyday Life in the Modern World*, trans. Sacha Rabinovitch, p. 202.
3. Stevens, *Collected Poems*, p. 43.
4. William Carlos Williams, *Paterson*, p. 103. Hereafter page numbers will be cited in the text.
5. Frank O'Hara, "Statement on Poetics," in *The New American Poetry*, ed. Donald Allen, pp. 419–420. Reprinted in

The Collected Poems of Frank O'Hara, ed. Donald Allen, p. 500.

6. Harold Rosenberg, "The American Action Painters," in his *The Tradition of the New*, p. 28.

7. William Carlos Williams, in the Preface to *Profile of William Carlos Williams*, ed. Jerome Mazzaro, p. iii.

8. William Carlos Williams, "The Basis of Faith in Art," in *Selected Essays of William Carlos Williams*, p. 194. Hereafter references to *Selected Essays* will be cited in the text as *SE*, followed by the page number.

9. Williams, in *Profile of William Carlos Williams*, p. iii.

10. See, e.g., Mike Weaver, *William Carlos Williams*, p. 99.

11. The history of avant-gardism and its initial alliance with political radicalism would bear Williams out. For example, it was the Russian avant-garde that sided with the early Bolsheviks, while the realists sided with the bourgeoisie. Indeed, it is realism—the product of bourgeois culture—that is reactionary, insofar as it tends to naturalize a social system and to blur the distinction between the way things are and the way they could or should be. Consequently, to consider social realism the art of the masses is to choose to ignore its uses as a bureaucratically imposed *ideology*. (See, e.g., Abram Tertz [Andrei Simiavskii], *On Socialist Realism*, trans. George Dennis.) In this way, not only is realism—which *is* a historical product—misunderstood, but history itself is robbed of its essence of change. Thus the communist ideologue is not much different from the bourgeois, for as Roland Barthes has argued, it is precisely a bourgeois trick to make what is a historical situation appear natural or of the essence of the universe, so that "bourgeois norms are experienced as the evident laws of a natural order." See "Myth Today," in *Mythologies*, trans. Annette Lavers, p. 140.

12. Barthes, "Myth Today," p. 139.

13. Harold Rosenberg, "The Avant-Garde," in his *Discovering the Present*, pp. 85, 76.

14. Ibid., p. 79.

15. Once again, this development has its political analog, for each revolutionary change in history involves expanding the definition of free citizenship.

16. William Carlos Williams, *The Autobiography of William Carlos Williams*, pp. 391–392.

17. William Carlos Williams, *Spring and All*, in his *Imaginations*, ed. Webster Schott, p. 90.

18. See William Carlos Williams, "To Elsie," in *The Collected Earlier Poems of William Carlos Williams*, pp. 270–272.

19. William Carlos Williams, "Raleigh Was Right," in *The Collected Later Poems of William Carlos Williams*, p. 52.

20. Williams would agree with urban theorists like Lewis Mumford and Henri Lefebvre that the city is the locus of the drama of modern life. See Mumford, *The Culture of Cities*, p. 481; and Lefebvre, *Everyday Life in the Modern World*, pp. 190–191. *Paterson* is full of the kind of chance encounters that only a city can provide, perhaps the most stunning being Williams's meeting the thin, old woman in Bk. 5. Through such encounters, one retains a sense of life as *drama*, which is precisely a sense of life as a creative and self-creative process.

21. The radical goal of Williams's poetry—the regeneration of everyday life—closely resembles the sort of revolution that a Marxist like Lefebvre envisions: "The revival of art and of the meaning of art has a practical not a 'cultural' aim; indeed, our cultural revolution has no purely 'cultural' aims, but directs culture towards experience, towards the transfiguration of everyday life. The revolution will transform existence, not merely the state and the distribution of property, for we do not take means for ends. This can also be stated as follows: 'Let everyday life become a work of art! Let every technical means be employed for the transformation of everyday life!' From an intellectual point of view the word 'creation' will no longer be restricted to works of art but will signify a self-conscious activity, self-conceiving, reproducing its own terms, adapting these terms and its own reality (body, desire, time, space), being its own creation; socially the term will stand for the activity of a collectivity assuming the responsibility of its own social function and destiny—in other words for *self-administration*" (*Everyday Life in the Modern World*, p. 204).

22. Bram Dijkstra, *The Hieroglyphics of a New Speech*, pp. 48–49.

23. Jerome Mazzaro, *William Carlos Williams*, p. 53. On the kinds of prose in *Paterson* and Williams's method of counterpointing, see Ralph Nash, "The Use of Prose in *Pater-*

son," *Perspective* 6, no. 4 (Autumn–Winter 1953): 191–199.

24. Mazzaro, *William Carlos Williams*, pp. 25–26.

25. Harold Rosenberg, "The Philosophy of Put-Togethers," *New Yorker*, March 11, 1972, p. 117.

26. William Carlos Williams, *The Selected Letters of William Carlos Williams*, ed. John C. Thirlwall, p. 263.

27. Daniel-Henry Kahnweiler, *Juan Gris*, trans. Douglas Cooper, p. 124.

28. Rosenberg, *Discovering the Present*, p. 75.

29. Louis Martz, "The Unicorn in *Paterson*: William Carlos Williams," *Thought* 35, no. 136 (Winter 1960): 543.

30. Williams, *The Selected Letters*, p. xvii.

31. Alain Jouffroy, "Will the Future Abolish Art?" trans. Roger Greaves, in *Figurative Art since 1945*, by J. P. Hodin et al., p. 304.

32. William Carlos Williams, "January Morning," in *The Collected Earlier Poems*, pp. 165–166.

33. Poe, "The Philosophy of Composition," p. 455. In the latter sense, collages are radically historical in that they literally age; e.g., the newspaper pieces that Picasso and Gris used in their collages are now disintegrating. Williams's use of "dated" prose and "timeless" poetry represents an analogous counterpointing.

34. Marcel Duchamp, in *Dialogues with Marcel Duchamp*, by Pierre Cabanne, ed. Robert Motherwell, trans. Ron Padgett, p. 67.

35. "The Editors Meet William Carlos Williams," *A.D. 1952* 3 (Winter 1952): 13.

36. Jouffroy, "Will the Future Abolish Art?" p. 303.

37. William Carlos Williams, *I Wanted to Write a Poem*, ed. Edith Heal, p. 82.

38. O'Hara, *The Collected Poems*, p. 398. Subsequent references will be cited in the text as *CP*.

39. Frank O'Hara, "Personism: A Manifesto," in *The Collected Poems*, p. 498.

40. Harold Rosenberg, "Action Painting: Crisis and Distortion," in his *The Anxious Object*, p. 46.

41. Frank O'Hara, "Larry Rivers: A Memoir," in *The Collected Poems*, p. 515.

42. Frank O'Hara, in Bill Berkson, "Frank O'Hara and His Poems," *Art and Literature*, no. 12 (Spring 1967): 53.

43. O'Hara, "Statement on Poetics," p. 500.
44. O'Hara, "Personism," p. 498.
45. Kenneth Koch, "All the Imagination Can Hold," *New Republic*, January 1, 1972, p. 24.
46. Frank O'Hara, "About Zhivago and His Poems," in *The Collected Poems*, p. 493.
47. Frank O'Hara, *Jackson Pollock*, pp. 21–22.
48. Kahnweiler, *Juan Gris*, p. 184.
49. John Ashbery, Introduction to *The Collected Poems*, p. vii.
50. Koch, "All the Imagination Can Hold," p. 24.
51. Stevens, *Collected Poems*, p. 250.
52. Koch, "All the Imagination Can Hold," p. 24.
53. Kenneth Burke, "Antony in Behalf of the Play," in his *The Philosophy of Literary Form*, pp. 279–290.

Sources Cited

Aaron, Daniel. "The Treachery of Recollection: The Inner and the Outer History." In *Essays on History and Literature*, edited by Robert H. Bremner, pp. 1–27. Columbus: Ohio State University Press, 1966.

Adams, Henry. "Buddha and Brahma." *Yale Review* 5, no. 1 (October 1915): 82–89.

———. *A Cycle of Adams Letters: 1861–1865*. Edited by Worthington Chauncey Ford. 2 vols. Boston: Houghton Mifflin, 1920.

———. *Democracy*. New York: New American Library, 1961.

———. *The Education of Henry Adams*. Boston: Houghton Mifflin, 1918.

———. *Letters of Henry Adams (1858–1891)*. Edited by Worthington Chauncey Ford. Boston: Houghton Mifflin, 1930.

———. *Letters of Henry Adams (1892–1918)*. Edited by Worthington Chauncey Ford. Boston: Houghton Mifflin, 1938.

Allen, Donald, ed. *The New American Poetry*. New York: Grove, 1960.

Allen, Gay Wilson. "Biblical Analogies for Walt Whitman's Prosody." *Revue Anglo-Américaine* 10, no. 6 (August 1933): 490–507.

———. *The Solitary Singer: A Critical Biography of Walt Whitman*. New York: New York University Press, 1967.

Anderson, Charles R. *The Magic Circle of Walden*. New York: Holt, Rinehart & Winston, 1968.

Anderson, Quentin. *The Imperial Self: An Essay in American Literary and Cultural History*. New York: Knopf, 1971.

Ashbery, John. Introduction. In *The Collected Poems of Frank O'Hara*, edited by Donald Allen, pp. vii–xi. New York: Knopf, 1971.

Asselineau, Roger. *The Evolution of Walt Whitman: The Creation of a Personality*. Translated by Richard P. Adams. Cambridge: Harvard University Press, 1960.

Augustine, Saint. *Confessions*. Translated by R. S. Pine-Coffin. Baltimore: Penguin, 1961.

Barthes, Roland. "Action Sequences." In *Patterns of Literary*

Style, edited by Joseph P. Strelka, pp. 5–14. University Park: Pennsylvania State University Press, 1971.

———. *Mythologies*. Translated by Annette Lavers. New York: Hill & Wang, 1960.

———. *Writing Degree Zero*. Translated by Annette Lavers and Colin Smith. New York: Hill & Wang, 1968.

Baym, Max I. "Henry Adams and the Critics." *American Scholar* 15, no. 1 (Winter 1945–46): 79–89.

Becker, Carl L. *Everyman His Own Historian: Essays on History and Politics*. New York: Appleton, 1935.

Bergson, Henri, and George Meredith. *Comedy: Two Classic Studies*. Edited with an introduction by Wylie Sypher. Garden City: Doubleday, 1956.

Berkson, Bill. "Frank O'Hara and His Poems." *Art and Literature*, no. 12 (Spring 1967): 53–63.

Blackmur, R. P. *The Expense of Greatness*. Gloucester: Peter Smith, 1958.

———. "In the Country of the Blue." *Kenyon Review* 5, no. 4 (Autumn 1943): 595–617.

———, ed. Introduction. In *The Art of the Novel*, by Henry James, pp. vii–xxxix. New York: Scribner's, 1934.

Borges, Jorge Luis. *Other Inquisitions:1937–1952*. Translated by Ruth L. C. Simms. Austin: University of Texas Press, 1964.

Burgess, C. F. "The Seeds of Art: Henry James's *Donnée*." *Literature and Psychology* 8, no. 3 (Summer 1963): 67–73.

Burke, Kenneth. *Attitudes toward History*. Boston: Beacon, 1961.

———. *Language as Symbolic Action: Essays on Life, Literature, and Method*. Berkeley & Los Angeles: University of California Press, 1968.

———. *Permanence and Change: An Anatomy of Purpose*. Indianapolis: Bobbs-Merrill, 1965.

———. *The Philosophy of Literary Form: Studies in Symbolic Action*. New York: Random House, 1957.

———. "Policy Made Personal." In *Leaves of Grass: One Hundred Years After*, edited by Milton Hindus, pp. 74–108. Stanford: Stanford University Press, 1955.

Cabanne, Pierre. *Dialogues with Marcel Duchamp*. Edited by Robert Motherwell. Translated by Ron Padgett. New York: Viking, 1971.

Carlyle, Thomas. *The Collected Works of Thomas Carlyle*. 26 vols. Boston: Dana Estes & Co., n.d.

Cassirer, Ernst. *Language and Myth*. Translated by Susanne K. Langer. New York: Dover, 1953.

————. *Mythical Thought*. Vol. 2 of *The Philosophy of Symbolic Forms*. Translated by Ralph Manheim. New Haven: Yale University Press, 1955.

Cater, Harold Dean, ed. *Henry Adams and His Friends*. Boston: Houghton Mifflin, 1947.

Cornford, Francis. *The Origin of Attic Comedy*. London: Arnold, 1914.

Cowley, Malcolm, ed. *Walt Whitman's Leaves of Grass: The First (1855) Edition*. New York: Viking, 1959.

de Selincourt, Basil. *Walt Whitman: A Critical Study*. Reprint of 1914 edition. New York: Russell, 1965.

Dickinson, Emily. *The Poems of Emily Dickinson*. Edited by Thomas H. Johnson. 3 vols. Cambridge: Harvard University Press, 1955.

Dijkstra, Bram. *The Hieroglyphics of a New Speech: Cubism, Stieglitz, and the Early Poetry of William Carlos Williams*. Princeton: Princeton University Press, 1969.

Edel, Leon. *Henry James: The Master 1901–1916*. Philadelphia: Lippincott, 1972.

"The Editors Meet William Carlos Williams." *A.D. 1952* 3 (Winter 1952): 5–14.

Emerson, Ralph Waldo. *The Complete Works of Ralph Waldo Emerson*. Edited by Edward Waldo Emerson. 12 vols. Boston: Houghton Mifflin, 1903–1904.

Fergusson, Francis. *The Idea of a Theater: A Study of Ten Plays, the Art of Drama in Changing Perspective*. Princeton: Princeton University Press, 1949.

Focillon, Henri. *The Life of Forms in Art*. Translated by Charles Beecher Hogan and George Kubler. New York: Wittenborn, 1948.

Freud, Sigmund. *Beyond the Pleasure Principle*. Edited and translated by James Strachey. New York: Bantam, 1959.

————. *Character and Culture*. Edited by Philip Rieff. New York: Collier, 1963.

————. *General Psychological Theory*. Edited by Philip Rieff. New York: Collier, 1963.

————. *Jokes and Their Relation to the Unconscious*. Translated by James Strachey. New York: Norton, 1963.

Frost, Robert. "Thoreau's *Walden.*" *The Listener,* August 26, 1954, pp. 319–320.

Hochfield, George. *Henry Adams: An Introduction and Interpretation.* New York: Barnes, 1962.

Husserl, Edmund. *The Phenomenology of Internal Time-Consciousness.* Edited by Martin Heidegger. Translated by James S. Churchill. Bloomington: Indiana University Press, 1964.

Iser, Wolfgang. "The Reading Process: A Phenomenological Approach." *New Literary History* 3, no. 2 (Winter 1972): 279–299.

James, Henry. *The Art of the Novel.* Edited by R. P. Blackmur. New York: Scribner's, 1934.

———. *The Letters of Henry James.* Edited by Percy Lubbock. 2 vols. New York: Scribner's, 1920.

———. *Partial Portraits.* London: Macmillan, 1919.

Jarrell, Randall. *Poetry and the Age.* New York: Knopf, 1953.

Johnson, Edgar. "Henry Adams: The Last Liberal." *Science and Society* 1, no. 3 (Spring 1937): 362–377.

Jordy, William H. *Henry Adams: Scientific Historian.* New Haven: Yale University Press, 1952.

Jouffroy, Alain. "Will the Future Abolish Art?" Translated by Roger Greaves. In *Figurative Art since 1945,* by J. P. Hodin et al., pp. 303–322. London: Thames & Hudson, 1971.

Jung, C. G. *Aion: Researches into the Phenomenology of the Self.* Translated by R. F. C. Hull. New York: Pantheon, 1959.

Kahnweiler, Daniel-Henry. *Juan Gris: His Life and Work.* Translated by Douglas Cooper. 2d ed. London: Thames & Hudson, 1969.

Kazin, Alfred. "Autobiography as Narrative." *Michigan Quarterly Review* 3, no. 4 (Fall 1964): 210–216.

Kierkegaard, Søren. *The Journals of Søren Kierkegaard.* Edited and translated by Alexander Dru. London: Oxford University Press, 1938.

———. *Repetition: An Essay in Experimental Psychology.* Translated by Walter Lowrie. New York: Harper & Row, 1941.

Kinnaird, John. "*Leaves of Grass* and the American Paradox." In *Whitman: A Collection of Critical Essays,* edited by Roy Harvey Pearce, pp. 24–36. Englewood Cliffs: Prentice-Hall, 1962.

Kirsch, James. *Shakespeare's Royal Self*. New York: Putnam, 1966.

Knight, G. Wilson. *The Wheel of Fire*. Cleveland: World, 1957.

Koch, Kenneth. "All the Imagination Can Hold." *New Republic*, January 1, 1972, p. 24.

Kronenberger, Louis. "The Education of Henry Adams." In *Books That Changed Our Minds*, edited by Malcolm Cowley and Bernard Smith, pp. 45–57. New York: Doubleday, 1939.

Krutch, Joseph Wood. *Henry David Thoreau*. New York: Sloane, 1948.

Langbaum, Robert. *The Poetry of Experience: The Dramatic Monologue in Modern Literary Tradition*. New York: Norton, 1957.

Langer, Susanne K. *Philosophy in a New Key: A Study in the Symbolism of Reason, Rite, and Art*. New York: New American Library, 1951.

Lawrence, D. H. *The Collected Letters of D. H. Lawrence*. Edited by Harry T. Moore. 2 vols. London: Heinemann, 1962.

—————. *Studies in Classic American Literature*. New York: Viking, 1961.

Lefebvre, Henri. *Everyday Life in the Modern World*. Translated by Sacha Rabinovitch. New York: Harper & Row, 1971.

Levenson, J. C. *The Mind and Art of Henry Adams*. Boston: Houghton Mifflin, 1957.

Lewis, R. W. B. *Trials of the Word: Essays in American Literature and the Humanistic Tradition*. New Haven: Yale University Press, 1965.

Lowell, James Russell. *The Writings of James Russell Lowell*. 10 vols. Boston: Houghton Mifflin, 1913.

Lurie, Edward. "American Scholarship: A Subjective Interpretation of Nineteenth-Century Cultural History." In *Essays on History and Literature*, edited by Robert H. Bremner, pp. 31–80. Columbus: Ohio State University Press, 1966.

Lynen, John F. *The Design of the Present: Essays on Time and Form in American Literature*. New Haven: Yale University Press, 1969.

McCarthy, Mary. "A Guide to Exiles, Expatriates, and Internal

Emigrés." *New York Review of Books*, March 9, 1972, pp. 4–8.

Marcuse, Herbert. *Eros and Civilization*. New York: Random House, 1955.

Martz, Louis. "The Unicorn in *Paterson*: William Carlos Williams." *Thought* 35, no. 136 (Winter 1960): 537–554.

Matthiessen, F. O. *American Renaissance: Art and Expression in the Age of Emerson and Whitman*. New York: Oxford University Press, 1941.

Mazzaro, Jerome. *William Carlos Williams: The Later Poems*. Ithaca: Cornell University Press, 1973.

———, ed. *Profile of William Carlos Williams*. Columbus: Charles E. Merrill, 1971.

Melville, Herman. *Moby-Dick*. Edited by Charles Feidelson, Jr. Indianapolis: Bobbs-Merrill, 1964.

Merleau-Ponty, Maurice. *Signs: Studies in Phenomenology and Existential Philosophy*. Translated by Richard C. McCleary. Evanston: Northwestern University Press, 1964.

Miller, Edwin Haviland. *Walt Whitman's Poetry: A Psychological Journey*. New York: New York University Press, 1968.

Miller, J. Hillis. "The Geneva School: The Criticism of Marcel Raymond, Albert Béguin, Georges Poulet, Jean Rousset, Jean-Pierre Richard, and Jean Starobinski." In *Modern French Criticism: From Proust and Valéry to Structuralism*, edited by John K. Simon, pp. 277–310. Chicago: University of Chicago Press, 1972.

Miller, Perry. "The Shaping of the American Character." *New England Quarterly* 28, no. 4 (December 1955): 435–454.

Misch, Georg. *A History of Autobiography in Antiquity*. Translated by E. W. Dickes. 2 vols. Cambridge: Harvard University Press, 1951.

Moldenhauer, Joseph J. "Paradox in *Walden*." In *Twentieth Century Interpretations of Walden*, edited by Richard Ruland, pp. 73–84. Englewood Cliffs: Prentice-Hall, 1968.

Muecke, Douglas C. *The Compass of Irony*. London: Methuen, 1969.

Mumford, Lewis. *The Culture of Cities*. New York: Harcourt, Brace, 1938.

Nash, Ralph. "The Use of Prose in *Paterson*." *Perspective* 6, no. 4 (Autumn–Winter 1953): 191–199.

Nietzsche, Friedrich. *The Birth of Tragedy and the Genealogy of Morals*. Translated by Francis Golffing. Garden City: Doubleday, 1956.

O'Hara, Frank. *The Collected Poems of Frank O'Hara*. Edited by Donald Allen. New York: Knopf, 1971.
———. *Jackson Pollock*. New York: Braziller, 1959.
Ovid. *The Metamorphoses*. Translated by Horace Gregory. New York: New American Library, 1960.
Pascal, Roy. *Design and Truth in Autobiography*. London: Routledge & Kegan Paul, 1960.
Paterson, John. "The Language of 'Adventure' in Henry James." *American Literature* 32, no. 3 (November 1960): 291–301.
Paul, Sherman. *The Shores of America: Thoreau's Inward Exploration*. Urbana: University of Illinois Press, 1958.
Pearce, Roy Harvey. *The Continuity of American Poetry*. Princeton: Princeton University Press, 1967.
Poe, Edgar Allan. *The Complete Works of Edgar Allan Poe*. Edited by James A. Harrison. 17 vols. Reprint of 1902 edition. New York: AMS Press, 1965.
Poulet, Georges. "Phenomenology of Reading." *New Literary History* 1, no. 1 (Fall 1969): 53–68.
———. *Studies in Human Time*. Translated by Elliott Coleman. Baltimore: Johns Hopkins Press, 1956.
Robbe-Grillet, Alain. *For a New Novel: Essays on Fiction*. Translated by Richard Howard. New York: Grove, 1965.
Roelofs, Gerrit H. "Henry Adams: Pessimism and the Intelligent Use of Doom." *ELH* 17, no. 3 (September 1950): 214–239.
Romberg, Bertil. *Studies in the Narrative Technique of the First-Person Novel*. Translated by Michael Taylor and Harold H. Borland. Stockholm: Almqvist & Wiksell, 1962.
Rosenberg, Harold. *The Anxious Object: Art Today and Its Audience*. New York: Collier, 1964.
———. *Discovering the Present: Three Decades in Art, Culture, and Politics*. Chicago: University of Chicago Press, 1973.
———. "The Philosophy of Put-Togethers." *New Yorker*, March 11, 1972, pp. 117–122.
———. *The Tradition of the New*. New York: McGraw-Hill, 1965.
Samuels, Ernest. *Henry Adams: The Major Phase*. Cambridge: Harvard University Press, 1964.
Sartre, Jean-Paul. *Nausea*. Translated by Lloyd Alexander. Norfolk: New Directions, 1959.
———. *The Philosophy of Jean-Paul Sartre*. Edited by Robert D. Cumming. New York: Random House, 1965.

Sayre, Robert F. *The Examined Self: Benjamin Franklin, Henry Adams, Henry James*. Princeton: Princeton University Press, 1964.

Shanley, J. Lyndon. *The Making of* Walden. Chicago: University of Chicago Press, 1957.

Skwire, David. "A Check List of Wordplays in *Walden*." *American Literature* 31, no. 3 (November 1959): 282–289.

Spender, Stephen. *The Making of a Poem*. London: Hamilton, 1955.

Starobinski, Jean. "The Style of Autobiography." In *Literary Style: A Symposium*, edited and translated by Seymour Chatman, pp. 285–296. London: Oxford University Press, 1971.

Stein, Gertrude. *Narration: Four Lectures*. Chicago: University of Chicago Press, 1969.

Stevens, Wallace. *The Collected Poems of Wallace Stevens*. New York: Knopf, 1954.

Sypher, Wylie. *Rococo to Cubism in Art and Literature*. New York: Vintage, 1960.

Tertz, Abram [Andrei Simiavskii]. *On Socialist Realism*. Translated by George Dennis. New York: Pantheon, 1960.

Thoreau, Henry David. *Consciousness in Concord: The Text of Thoreau's Hitherto "Lost Journal," 1840–1841*. Edited by Perry Miller. Boston: Houghton Mifflin, 1958.

———. *The Correspondence of Henry David Thoreau*. Edited by Walter Harding and Carl Bode. New York: New York University Press, 1958.

———. *Walden*. Edited by J. Lyndon Shanley. Princeton: Princeton University Press, 1971.

———. *The Writings of Henry David Thoreau*. Edited by Bradford Torrey. 20 vols. Boston: Houghton Mifflin, 1906.

Valéry, Paul. *The Art of Poetry*. Translated by Denise Folliot. New York: Random House, 1958.

Vandersee, Charles. "The Four Menageries of Henry Adams." *Arizona Quarterly* 24, no. 4 (Winter 1968): 293–308.

———. "The Hamlet in Henry Adams." In *Shakespeare Survey*, vol. 24, edited by Kenneth Muir, pp. 87–104. Cambridge: Cambridge University Press, 1971.

Weaver, Mike. *William Carlos Williams: The American Background*. Cambridge: Cambridge University Press, 1971.

Wellek, René. *The Later Nineteenth Century*. Vol. 4 of *A History of Modern Criticism 1750–1950*. New Haven: Yale University Press, 1965.

Whitman, Walt. *The Collected Prose*. Vol. 2 of *The Works of Walt Whitman*. New York: Minerva, 1969.
———. *Leaves of Grass*. Edited by Harold W. Blodgett and Sculley Bradley. New York: Norton, 1968.
Willeford, William. *The Fool and His Scepter: A Study in Clowns and Jesters and Their Audience*. Evanston: Northwestern University Press, 1969.
Williams, William Carlos. *The Autobiography of William Carlos Williams*. New York: New Directions, 1951.
———. *The Collected Earlier Poems of William Carlos Williams*. Norfolk: New Directions, 1951.
———. *The Collected Later Poems of William Carlos Williams*. Norfolk: New Directions, 1950.
———. *Imaginations*. Edited by Webster Schott. New York: New Directions, 1951.
———. *I Wanted to Write a Poem*. Edited by Edith Heal. Boston: Beacon, 1958.
———. *Paterson*. New York: New Directions, 1963.
———. *Selected Essays of William Carlos Williams*. New York: New Directions, 1969.
———. *The Selected Letters of William Carlos Williams*. Edited by John C. Thirlwall. New York: McDowell, Obolensky, 1957.
Winters, Yvor. *In Defense of Reason*. Denver: Swallow, 1937.
Wordsworth, William, and Dorothy Wordsworth. *The Early Letters of William and Dorothy Wordsworth (1787–1805)*. Edited by Ernest de Selincourt. Oxford: Clarendon, 1935.
Zweig, Paul. *The Heresy of Self-Love: A Study of Subversive Individualism*. New York: Harper & Row, 1968.

Index

Aaron, Daniel, 70
Action Painting, 117, 145
Adams, Henry: and anticipation, xx, 90–91, 93, 94, 100, 109; and Saint Augustine, 82, 110; and comedy, 97, 98, 102–104, 108, 111; as conservative anarchist, 107–108; and contradiction, 79–82, 101; and Dante, 82, 107; as dispossessed heir, 82, 96; on education, 79, 84, 85, 102–103, 105; as failure, 100, 169–170n; as fool, 95–97; as future-oriented, 85, 91; and Hamlet, 82–85, 88–90, 94, 95–96, 100, 106, 107, 108, 168–169n; and history, xviii, 92, 97–100; irony of, 88–89, 101–102, 109; and James, 100, 104, 109; mixed interests of, 81–82; and narcissism, 99–100; and Narcissus, 84; and power, 85–90; and repetition as mastery, xix, xxi, 86, 109; and self-consciousness, 84, 96, 102–104; solipsism of, 99–100; as suicidal, 81, 84, 90–91, 93–94, 96, 99, 107; theory of history of, 94, 99, 100–102; and Thoreau, 90, 94, 100; and time, 83, 85, 91–93, 100; and Whitman, 91, 100. *Works: Democracy*, 87, 89; *The Education of Henry Adams*: as autobiography, 98, 104, 109–111; as class rhetoric, 86, 109; as comedy, xxviii, 97–98, 102–108, 111; death in, 90–91, 105; double perspective in, xxvii, 98–100, 103, 104; influence on historiography of, 85–86, 89, 109; insect imagery in, 101; literary models for, xiii, 82; point of view in, 98–100, 103, 104; rebirth patterns in, 105–107; rhetoric of realism in, 89–90; as strategy for living, 102–103, 109; as suicidal, xiv–xv, 90–91, 93–94, 98–99, 110
Allen, Gay Wilson, 44, 47, 50
Anderson, Charles R., 11
Anderson, Quentin, 37, 75
Anticipation: in Adams, xx, 90–91, 93, 94, 100, 109; as mastery, xx–xxi; as protective strategy, 90–91, 95, 100; in Thoreau, xx, 13, 19, 20; in Whitman, xx, 47
Arensberg, Walter, 119
Ashbery, John, 147
Asselineau, Roger, 34, 47, 50
Augustine, Saint, xiii, xxvii, 6, 72, 82, 110
Autobiographical literature, xi, xiii, xiv, 3, 4, 29, 50, 51, 57, 65, 70–71, 74–75; as

action, xviii, 65–66, 116–
117, 132–133; and the
American experience, xi–
xiii, 157; as comic, xxvii–
xxviii, 103–104; as conversion of history and form,
xiii–xvi; creative power of,
xii, 157–160; as death, xx,
xxi, 93–94, 150–151; didacticism of, xii; double perspective in, xxvi–xxviii, 27,
103; as event, xv–xviii, xxi–
xxiii, xxvi; and fiction, 3,
4, 66–67, 69, 162n; hero in,
xiv–xv, xxvii, 7, 20–21, 29,
49, 72, 73–74, 103; and
history, xvi–xix, xxi–xxv;
innovativeness of, 133, 160;
narcissism of, xxi, 6; open-
endedness of, xxv, 93, 133;
point of view in, xxvi
xxviii, 65, 67–69, 98, 103–
104; political power of, xiii,
158; and the reader, xxvi,
3–4, 7, 76; as repetition,
xviii–xxi, xxviii; as resurrection, xxi, 106; as ritual,
xvii–xviii, xxvi; self as form
in, xiii, xiv; and self-
consciousness, xiii–xiv,
xxvi–xxvii, 6–7, 103–104;
as strategy for living, xviii,
xix; style in, xiii, xv, 49, 70,
160; time in, xx, xxii, xxiv–
xxv, 3, 23
Avant-garde, 120, 121–122,
133–134, 172n

Barthes, Roland, xx, 63, 68,
121, 172n
Bergson, Henri, 79–80
Blackmur, R. P., 74
Borges, Jorge Luis, 51

Burke, Kenneth, 10, 34, 79–
80, 81, 89, 107, 155

Carlyle, Thomas, 103
Cassirer, Ernst, 28–29, 30
Channing, Ellery, 21
Comedy, 97, 98, 103, 105,
107, 108, 111
Cornford, Francis, 107
Cowley, Malcolm, 48, 50
Crane, Hart, 123
Cubist poets, 145
Cummings, E. E., 134–135

Dante Alighieri, xiii, 82, 107
De Selincourt, Basil, 44, 46
Dickinson, Emily, 110
Dijkstra, Bram, 129
Doubleness: in Adams, 80–81,
84, 98, 100, 103, 104; in
autobiography, xxvi xxviii,
27, 103; in James, xxvii,
xxviii; in Thoreau, xxvii,
9–11; in Whitman, xxvii–
xxviii, 36–37
Duchamp, Marcel, xxii, 138

Economy, 16, 17, 23; in
James, 60, 65, 73; and
narcissism, 8; in Thoreau,
12–17
Edwards, Jonathan, xi–xii
Eliot, T. S., 123, 131
Emerson, Ralph Waldo, 5, 8,
14, 15, 34, 74, 119
Everyday life, 115–116, 173n;
and avant-garde art, 115,
117; in O'Hara, 115–117,
141–142, 143, 147; in Williams, 115–117, 122–124,
173n

Fergusson, Francis, 96, 108

Focillon, Henri, xxiii
Fools, 95–96
Franklin, Benjamin, xi–xii, 157. *Work: The Autobiography of Benjamin Franklin*, xiii, 3, 157
Freud, Sigmund, xix, xxi, 9, 16, 38, 99, 102
Frost, Robert, 19–20

Ginsberg, Allen, 132, 135–136

Hawthorne, Nathaniel, xiii
Hay, John, 100
Hemingway, Ernest, 158–159
Hero: Adams as, 82, 96–100, 103–105; in autobiographical literature, xiv–xv, xxvii, 7, 20–21, 29, 49, 72, 73–74, 103; James as, 72–74, 75; as representative, xiv, 21, 73–74; Thoreau as, 7–8, 20–21; Whitman as, 28–30, 36, 49–50
Husserl, Edmund, 69

Identity-in-difference, 9–12, 16, 17
Irony, 88, 101–102; in Adams, 88–89, 101–102, 109; in Thoreau, 14
Iser, Wolfgang, 62–63

James, Henry: and compositional centers, 60, 61; and consciousness, 72, 76; and the distortions of style, 70; on economy, 60, 65, 73; mirror imagery, use of, 75; past in, 69; on reading, 62–63; and repetition as mastery, xix, xx–xxi, 74; and retrospection, 58–59, 61– 63, 65, 67–70; revisions of novels, 57, 61–63, 70; and Thoreau, 64, 74; and Whitman, 64, 74, 75. *Works: The Ambassadors*, 59, 61, 69, 71; *The American*, 61; "The Jolly Corner," 167n; Prefaces: adventure imagery in, 71–72; as autobiography, 57–58, 63–66, 72– 75; as criticism, 57, 70, 166n; double perspective in, xxvii, xxviii; as fiction, 57, 66–67; literary models for, xiii; organic imagery in, 58; point of view in, 58–59, 61– 63, 65, 67–68; self-consciousness in, xiv, 58– 61, 62, 64–65, 72–74
Jarrell, Randall, 38
Jordy, William, 88
Jouffroy, Alain, 133, 138
Jung, Carl, 36–37

Kahnweiler, Daniel-Henry, 131, 145
Kazin, Alfred, 4
Kierkegaard, Søren, 74, 88
Kinnaird, John, 50
Kirsch, James, 90
Knight, G. Wilson, 90
Koch, Kenneth, 144, 147, 155
Krutch, Joseph Wood, 15

Langbaum, Robert, 27, 28
Langer, Susanne K., xviii, 29
Lawrence, D. H., xix, 39
Lefebvre, Henri, 115, 173n
Levenson, J. C., 92
Lewis, R. W. B., 34
Literature: as communication, xvii, 134–135; as event, xv– xvi; as historical, xvii,

xxii–xxv, 23, 52–53, 137–
138; and history, xvii–xix,
xx, xxii, xxiii–xxiv, 52–53;
as ritual, xvii, xviii, xxvi;
and tradition, xiii–xiv, 161n
Lowell, James Russell, 8, 9, 21
Lurie, Edward, 85–86
Lynen, John, 33, 41

McCarthy, Mary, 73
Marcuse, Herbert, 9
Martz, Louis, 132
Matthiessen, F. O., 33, 37
Mazzaro, Jerome, 129–130
Melville, Herman, xiii, 6
Memory, 69–70; as creative,
159; distortions of, 70
Merleau-Ponty, Maurice, xv,
xvi, 98
Miller, Edwin H., 37, 47
Miller, Perry, 12–13, 17, 19, 51
Misch, Georg, 51
Moldenhauer, Joseph, 14
Mythic consciousness, 28–30;
in Whitman, 29–31

Narcissism, xxi, 8–9, 99–100
Narcissus, xxi, 5, 6, 8, 9, 10,
11, 12, 20, 84; and Adams,
84; and Melville, 6; and
Thoreau, 5, 8, 9, 10, 12, 20
Narrative, xx, xxii, 66–69;
distortions of, 70; time in,
xxii, 67–69
Newman, Barnett, 157
Nietzsche, Friedrich, 36, 47

O'Hara, Frank: on the attitude of attention, 143–146;
on the creative state, 145–
146; double perspective in,
xxviii; and everyday life,
115–117, 141–142, 143,

147; and impure poetry,
139–141; and the poem as
event, xxiii; on poetry as
drama, 140–141, 151, 153–
155; on poetry and life, 141,
142–144, 147–151; on
poetry and love, 152–155;
and poetry and personality,
155–156; and the reader,
155; and repetition as mastery, xix; and time, 149–
151, 154; and Whitman,
139, 140, 154, 155; and
Williams, 115–117, 139.
Works: "In Favor of One's
Time," 151–153; "In Mem-
ory of My Feelings," xxv,
147–151; "Personism," xxiii,
147, 153–154
Ovid, 6

Pascal, Roy, xx
Paul, Sherman, 10, 11
Perspective by incongruity,
79, 80
Poe, Edgar Allan, xiii, 10, 59,
135, 141
Point of view, in autobiog-
raphy, xxvi–xxviii, 65, 67–
69, 98, 103–104
Poulet, Georges, 8, 22, 69
Pound, Ezra, 118, 130
Puritan autobiography, xi–xii

Reading, xxvi, 3–4, 22, 23, 62–
63, 76; in James, 62–63; in
O'Hara, 155; in Thoreau,
22, 23; in Williams, 139
Realism, 90, 115
Repetition: in Adams, xix, xxi,
86, 109; and autobiography,
xviii–xxi, xxviii; as creative,
11–12, 158–159; and

doubleness, xxviii; economy of, 16–17; in James, 74; as mastery, xix–xxi, 74; representation as, 64, 67, 74; in Thoreau, 11–13, 15, 19; in Whitman, 33, 41–44. *See also* Anticipation

Repetition compulsion, xix, xxi

Retrospection, 58–59, 67–68; and comedy, 104; distortions of, 61–63, 69–70

Robbe-Grillet, Alain, xxv

Romantic poets, xxi, 28

Romberg, Bertil, 4

Rosenberg, Harold, xxii, 117, 121, 122, 130, 131, 142

Rousseau, Jean Jacques, xiii, 50

Sartre, Jean-Paul, xvi, 67

Satire, 89

Sayre, Robert, 105

Self: as form, xiii–xiv, 53, 72, 76, 136–137; as hero, xiv–xv, xxvii, 7, 21, 29, 49, 73–74, 103; as style, xiii, xv, 49, 160; as subject, xiv, 6, 103

Self-consciousness, 6, 7, 20–21; in Adams, 84, 96, 102–104; and autobiography, xiii–xiv, xxvi–xxvii, 6–7, 103–104; and comedy, 103; doubleness of, xxvi–xxvii, 9–10, 27, 84, 103; in James, 58–61, 62, 64–65, 72–74; as representative, xiv, 73–74; in Thoreau, 7, 9–10, 20–21; in Whitman, 27, 48

Shanley, J. Lyndon, 10, 17, 18

Shelley, Percy Bysshe, 151

Sincerity, xxvi, 49; in

Thoreau, 7; in Whitman, 49–50

Spender, Stephen, 103

Starobinski, Jean, xxvii, 49

Stein, Gertrude, 34, 129, 157–158

Stevens, Wallace, 74, 110, 115, 116, 142, 146, 152, 155

Style, in autobiographical literature, xiii, xv, 49, 70, 160

Subjectivity, 27–28

Sypher, Wylie, 97, 115

Thoreau, Henry David: and anticipation, xx, 13, 19, 20; and autobiography, 5, 7, 20; and Edwards, xi–xii; and Franklin, xii; and history, xviii; and narcissism, 8, 20; and Narcissus, 5, 8, 9, 10, 12, 20; and nature, 5, 14, 17; and repetition as mastery, xix, xx, xxi; and self-consciousness, 7, 9–10, 20–21; sincerity in, 7; style of, 15–16; and Whitman, 7, 20; and Wordsworth, 6–7. *Works: Journal*, 7, 8, 18; *Walden*: analogies in, 16–17; as autobiography, 3–5, 8, 19, 20–21; and *The Autobiography of Benjamin Franklin*, xii, 3; as comic, xxvii–xxviii; cyclical progression of, xiv, 11; doubleness in, xxvii, 9–11; economy of, 12–17; in history, xxiii–xxiv; mirror imagery in, 4–5; monetary imagery in, 13–14; mosaic method of, 18–19; and the reader, 22, 23; repetition in, 11–13,

15, 19; resurrection in, 5, 11–13, 19; revisions of, 3, 17–18; self-consciousness in, 7, 9–10, 20–21; symbolism in, 17; transcendence of time in, 19, 22–23; word plays in, 15–16

Valéry, Paul, 59, 68
Vandersee, Charles, 101

Whitman, Walt: and anticipation, xx, 47; and autobiography, 7, 20, 27, 29; as culture hero, 29; death wish of, 34–35; doubleness of, 36–37, 39; and Franklin, xii; and history, xviii–xix, 29–30, 50–53; as "kosmos," 36; political ideology of, 50–51; and repetition as mastery, xix, xx; as self-archetype, 36–39, 51; and self-consciousness, 27, 48; and Thoreau, 28, 47; universality of, 28, 36–39; and Wordsworth, 31, 39–40. Work: "Song of Myself": American context of, 29, 38, 50–52; as autobiography, 27, 44–47, 52; as biological autobiography, 33, 36; biological rhythms in, 30–36; as comic, xxviii; doubleness in, xxvii–xxviii, 44–49; evolutionary order of, xiv, xx, 41–43; evolution imagery in, 33, 42, 43; myth and history in, 29–30, 44–46, 49–53; as mythic auto-biography, 30, 36; mythic consciousness in, 28–29; point of view in, 39, 40, 43; repetition in, 33, 41–44; revisions of, 45–49, 50; structure of, 39–43; style of, 44; time in, 30, 35; and Walden, 46

Willeford, William, 95

Williams, William Carlos: and the city, 122–128, 173n; collage method of, 129, 130–132, 174n; and Cubism, 119, 129; and destruction as creation, 121–122, 127, 135–138; and everyday life, 115–117, 122–124, 173n; innovativeness of, 117–121; on memory, 159; on novelty, 118–119, 120, 122, 134; on poetry and society, 117–120, 122, 123, 128, 130–132, 134, 138; on poetry and time, 126–127; and repetition as mastery, xix; as social revolutionary, 118–121, 128, 139, 173n; and the "variable foot," 134, 138. Work: Paterson: as autobiography, 132–133, 135–137, 139; city as subject in, 122–128; as cultural autobiography, 122, 130, 136–137, 139; as cultural collaboration, 131–132; dissipation of energy in, 135–138; double perspective in, xxviii; historical structure of, xxv, 135–139; as impure poetry, xxv, 122, 129–132; prose and poetry in, 129–131; and time, 135, 137;

vulgarization of language in, 122, 129–132; vulgarization of structure in, 122, 132–138; vulgarization of subject in, 122–128

Wordsworth, William, 6–7, 31, 39–40
Wright, Richard, 158

Zweig, Paul, 20, 21

Blasing, Mutlu Konuk.

The art of life: studies in
American autobiographical
literature.